UNHITCHING
FROM BITCHING
LOVE LESSONS FOR PSYCHOTHERAPISTS

ALFRED FIREMAN, MD

ISBN: 978-0-9833376-3-8

Production Services:
Populore Publishing Company, Morgantown, West Virginia,
with cover design by Jenna Britton

Contents

Introduction

Many years ago I read a book titled "How to Live with a Neurotic." It proposed becoming a pseudo-psychiatrist advising the readers to give their neurotic partners space, or try to understand that they are not really angry with them even though it's the reader's life that the neurotics are making miserable.

How not to live with a neurotic and how to successfully leave a neurotic relationship is what this book is all about. It does not attempt to inspire by directing the reader to a superior power, nor does it provide physical or mental exercises to arouse a dormant or weak will to a higher efficiency. Most importantly, it makes no attempt to solve intrapersonal problems that involve only the reader, such as mood swings, overeating and stage fright. What it does is deal positively with your interpersonal problems, helping you to figure out why people behave the way they do with you and why you behave the way you do with them. Therefore, if you are tired of being bitched at in a losing relationship, or if you are the bitching partner and yearn to figure out why, then this book will take you step by step into the hidden complexity of the unconscious mind and reveal how, by its psychological mechanisms of defense, it can control your everyday interpersonal behavior. Such discoveries are often as painful as reassuring but choices can now be based upon a new appreciation of how complex our human connections really are but how accessible they are to insight and mastery.

This book does not begin with the premise that the reader is a likeable or lovable person. In fact it shows both your partner's and your limits in the interpersonal space in which you joust for connection to one another. It further states that while solving interpersonal problems is often worth the trouble, the alternative of ending a relationship may be the healthier thing to do. As you know far too well ending a relationship is frequently discouraged by marriage or couple counselors merely to keep clients/patients coming for "more work." I, however, have written this User's Manual on how to say goodbye to the folks with whom we are either mis- or malconnected and for whom we can wait no longer for things to get better with or without the approval of their therapists.

This book will identify the half-fact, half-fantasy, time-warped misconceptions that impair interpersonal relationships and then teach the reader how to exit in a healing way from those crazy connections in which distortion, displacement, despair and confusion prevail.

Insights derived from more than thirty years as a Board Certified Psychiatrist and Marriage Counselor will expose and resolve the troubled elements of the reader's relationships with spouses, lovers, friends, grown children and parents.

Critical chapters will be learned for exiting from such troubled relationships with this simple motto prevailing, i.e., that cannot be a fact of our interpersonal lives which is not a fact at all. What we mean by this can be simply demonstrated as follows: while no one may logically dispute the event that Joey says he loves Jane and feels or believes that it is true, the fact may be, and often is, that Joey does not love Jane. For the truth of love and the capacity to love does not equate to the ability to say so. Therefore, as soon as either of them accept that the magic of words must give way to the power of facts, the sooner do they begin their relationship in the real world.

Any child, fool, sociopath, or manipulator can say "I love you." Any charlatan or cheater in the games of love and getting can substitute words for meaning, symbols for facts and wishes for capacity or integrity.

Endurance and joy in interpersonal relationships, however, is not derived from hope or promise. Some folks do and some folks don't have the behavioral character traits and capacities which entitle them to pledge intimacy. Those who do, do not need to say "trust me"; they are trustworthy. Those who do, do not need to say "believe me"; they are reliable. Courtesy and kindness, cheer and helpfulness, predictability and loyalty abound in their yesterdays. Real world skills, aptitudes and performance are facts of their lives.

Psychological mechanisms of defense to thwart anxiety, avoid depressions or confound adversaries do not burden them.

By applying the lessons of this text to his sex, like and love life, the reader will also be emancipated from life's most seductive and dangerous word game and relieved of the paradoxes and ambivalence which haunt most love relationships. You will discover how your interpersonal life has prospered or failed on the basis of ideas rather than reality. You will see how entrapped you have become by oversimple or false premises about mind and persons. You will learn how critical misperceptions in these areas may freeze one's behavior into habit without choice. With this book, where intuition once prevailed, there shall intelligence and fact now reign.

You will now more precisely be able to define your irreconcilable interpersonal differences, and then transfer your caring energy to more deserving others. Less inclined to consider aberrant behavior as sickness, though not forsaking forgiveness in human relationships, you will also learn that to forgive is not to forbear. Discovery of those psychological bitching mechanisms which bind us to failure and thwart our natural propensity to achieve pleasure and relief of tension, enables you to stop repetitiously compulsive self-destructive, interpersonal behaviors. When these lessons are learned people will stop bringing the worst out of each other.

The reader will ultimately respect that reality, unencumbered by neurotic mechanisms of interpersonal defense, is the only place where genuinely happy human intercourse can occur. Neurotic people should get professional help. Relationships are tough enough without having to also be therapeutic.

Let's face it, we're no angels and folks can provoke folks to legitimately dislike them or be annoyed by them, but that's not bitching. If we are hostile, irreverent and uncouth, we invite legitimate disappointment and complaint. If we shouldn't have done what we did if it was insensitive, if it was hostile, then complaining about it by our partner is not bitching.

So, what is bitching? It is transference, a displacement, a projection of ideas, feelings, wishes, fears and confusions. It is redirecting ancient hurts and unresolved conflict into the here and now. That's why a psychiatrist is the most informed person to teach you about it for that's his stock in trade. Bitching is neurosis in action! Psychiatric therapy is an enterprise in understanding our ancient emotional history and by so doing exposing the psychological mechanisms of defense which, in our immature years, we fabricated to enable us to deal with our primal fears and uncertainties. The more we know about them the less necessary is it for us to adhere to them. The more we see them in our bitching partners, the clearer it becomes to us how they are controlled by these mechanisms and therefore more in need of therapy than hugging or, for that matter, forgiving, and certainly not forbearing.

Be warned, however, that understanding bitching mechanisms does not change the person bitching. As a matter of fact such understanding or interpretation is more often resented as a hostile invasion of privacy than appreciated as a helpful intervention. Also remember that understanding is neither judging nor caring. When others implore you to understand them, they very often presume that such understanding is a precondition to your accepting or loving them. They must be warned that this is not the case, for understanding merely increases your interpersonal options and, after reading this book your understanding may as often be a ticket out of a relationship as a reason for staying in one.

The theme and rationale for writing this book is this simple verity: that we are as vulnerable to neurotic injury in our intimate relationships as we are to outside injury by strangers. It has been a sad lesson of our middle and late years to have learned that human compatibility is not a trait acquired naturally but rather must be learned. This book hopes to accelerate this process by teaching the reader that no habit more impairs the joy of our existence than reliance on folk ways and myths and nature rather than science and knowledge to lead us on our interpersonal way.

It's too late to alter how we were reared. We are as potty-trained as we'll ever be. However, it is not too late to unhitch from the bitches who endure as testimony to our childish limitations in human relationships. When we learn that these relationships are as often based on fear of separating as on devotion, when we examine how we got into those relationships in the first place, we begin our journey out. Though we can't change the facts of our past, we can truly change how we respond to them. Nowhere else in their lives have my patients paid such a dear ransom for their existence than to have not appreciated this truth. Seldom, if ever, are the external facts of their lives as dangerous as the neurotic connections which bind them to their neurotic partners. Likewise, seldom, if ever, are here and now issues of pain and suffering as potent as those memories of past hurts which they excite.

Therefore, this psychiatrist will not favor inappropriate long-sufferingness as virtue or asset but will support the entitlement of his patients and his readers to leave neurotic, self-destructive relationships. "Forget it," I tell them, "if you are waiting for them to leave, because bitching partners can endure forever. The repetition compulsion will outlast the pleasure principle, every day of every week of their lives."

Buffered by the insights secured from this book, readers will learn that the true hazards that lie ahead for them in separation, exist only in themselves.

I know this because I also am an avid reader of psychological self-help books beginning with the works of Sheen, Overstreet, Carnegie and Liebmann, through the "I'm OK, You're OK" genre, and more recently Robin Norwood's "Women Who Love Too Much," Shere Hite's "Women and Love," and Susan Forward's "Men Who Hate Women and the Women Who Love Them." Their success clearly reveals folks' insatiable quest for understanding emotional problems and achieving satisfying personal relationships. But no one of them seems focused on, or appears to be cognizant of, the issues which I have just described, namely they are focused on your understanding you and your getting better with no follow up plan upon what to do next. The seduction of their titles and format reflect a simple premise: you'll feel better when you master the principles, subscribe to the philosophy or otherwise follow the directives of the author; your body and your perception of yourself will be more satisfying; your secret thoughts and wishes will be less reprehensible and your self-worth will surely improve.

The dialogue is between reader and author/teacher. The issue is "I don't feel nor fare well." The aim is to feel and fare better, and the method is self-awareness, with or without surrender to the power or the philosophy of the helper or of a higher power to whom you are directed. "Tell me," the reader beseeches in the private confessional of his library, "that you understand me, that you have seen such as me, that I am within the ken of your knowledge and science. Tell me that I am OK, not perverse or ugly, and not beyond reclamation. Reassure me that I am within the purview of a God who can forgive and/or a doctor who can cure. Most of all, show me that I am sexually adequate and personally loveable."

I know those folks that Shere Hite and Susan Forward are talking about, who are "extremely jealous and possessive; who switch from charm to anger without warning; who belittle their partner's opinions, their feelings, their accomplishment; who withdraw love, money, approval or sex to punish them and blame them for everything that goes wrong in their relationship." My book has one word for the long-suffering of such folks—LEAVE! My book simply conveys that it doesn't require a Ph.D. in psychology or an addiction to self-help books to realize that neurotic relationships feed upon themselves and that focusing upon the self or other, rather than the relationship, only delays the exit. For I can assure you that your partners will not leave you. They glom on to you with an interminable perseverance. But they do not "love" you too much, they hunger too much! Craving for affection and confirmation plays the same role in their lives as food, drink or drugs do in the lives of addicts. You are more like objects to be eaten than people to be encountered. Such immaturity however is not gender-specific, as the lady authors of those self-help books would have you believe.

My book shall surely remedy this by showing that complaining about the other while not looking at the relationship is a road to nowhere but more of the same. When wives of alcoholic husbands or husbands of alcoholic wives finish their litany of complaint about the abuse and perversions of purpose in their relationships, I say, as Portnoy's psychiatrist said to him, "now we can begin: we can now begin to look at what neurotic forces in your life fixes you so fastly to this person that you will convolute every principle of logic to sustain your status quo." The answer is simple to state, but enormously complex to surmount, namely that the repetition compulsion is a more potent factor in neurotic relationships than the pleasure principle which governs all other species, namely to seek satisfaction and avoid pain.

Any psychiatrist who has been paying careful attention to those thousands of patients whose therapy hours basically consist of bitching could have written this book. Few, however, would risk the financial jeopardy of renaming the condition and demedicalizing the solution. *Unhitching from Bitching* is specifically designed to do this, by sharing the insights of a psychiatrist who will provide techniques for resolving conflicted and low-yield, interpersonal experiences and strategies on how to end them! Psychiatric understanding can and should permit the option of ending neurotic relationships, a choice which often proves far more creative and self-fulfilling than stalemating in interminable therapy encounters. Where that kind of psychotherapy stalls, this book begins.

An analogy to the physicians of medieval Italy comes to mind. For centuries they limited forceps delivery to the aristocrats, while the peasants were allowed to tear their pelvises in "natural childbirth" without benefit of that scientific advance.

Likewise, today I believe the modern psychiatrist has the intellectual forceps to comprehend and provide more direct remedies for conflicted social relationships than tradition or bylaws have yet approved for general distribution.

Instead of sequestering those insights within the formal literature of his profession, or exclusively directing his efforts to the care of the ill, (often at the sacrifice of those who wait patiently at the bedside for the fevers of inappropriate anger or frozen sexuality to break), I believe the psychiatrist should go public with this pronouncement: what's good for many psychiatrists' patients may not be good for their families.

This author encourages his patients, their relatives, and now his readers, to at least consider this option. This book offers them in a focused and well-substantiated sequence of insights the knowledge and support that the only thing they have to fear in such a choice is the fear of being alone or not having each other. Upon realizing, however, that they never did "have each other," that what they had was a neurotic defensive relationship, the door for a better relationship, not worse, opens for both, either for a life together, or separately seeking other fortunes.

• • •

1

That Cannot Be a Fact of Love
Which Is Not a Fact at All

During a recent group therapy session, a new patient was talking about her boyfriend. "I really do love him," she began, but before her sentence could be completed, one of the veteran members interrupted. "Don't say love in this group," she admonished; "Dr. Fireman hates that word!"

Of course I do not hate that word, but I do hate what the misuse and abuse of that word does to players in the "I love you" word game. The saddest conclusion of my professional practice is that too many people who participate in this game are troubled or frightened players with no better way to connect to one another than through the magic, not the meaning, of words. In this chapter I shall explain the myriad fantasies that are generated by the word "love." Then I will suggest that, as soon as you know it isn't love, i.e., as soon as you know that saying it or feeling it does not make it so, as soon as you know that love can be validated and is provable, as soon as you know that loving is a skill to be mastered, not an instinct to be expressed, or a need to be sated, as soon as you know how to assign it to the reality and loveableness of your partner, then it becomes not only easier but rational and appropriate for you to leave such a relationship when love is not truly there.

The love word's ambiguity has led one clinician, Elvin Semrad, to consider love as a variety of mental illness, i.e., "the only socially accepted psychosis."

That love is clearly not true love but rather a child's game played by beginners in social intercourse with irreverent zeal and grandiosity. In those situations, the magic of the word love is mistaken for the meaning of the concept love and that is what Freud meant in his insightful aphorism when he said, "Words and magic were in the beginning one and the same thing and even today words retain much of their magical power."

This same originality of Freud in exposing the deceptive and magical power of words also accounts for his profoundly important essays on human sexuality. I shall now provide a brief review of these essays to serve as points of reference to clarify the often-tragic misunderstandings between love-making and sex-making.

Freud observed that human sexuality does not appear de-novo, from behind the curtain of pre-adolescence, fully formed and ready to articulate its timeless message. Rather, it is a process that begins in infancy, i.e., "It seems to be my fate to discover only the too obvious, that children have sexual feelings which every nursemaid knows."

He defines suckling and touching as early manifestations of a pervasive, polymorphous, human sexuality which eventually matures to adult, heterosexual, love relationship. He explained how this sexuality evolved through the oral, anal and genital stages of early childhood as the psychobiological loci where physical pleasure is most concentrated at those phases of development. More importantly, however, he showed the critical importance of the interpersonal events which were simultaneously occurring.

Freud's perception of the infant as sexually polymorphous rather than fully programmed and coded for its adult sexuality, provided a radical challenge to then prevailing, more simplistic notions. Namely that if creature needs, such as food and warmth, were provided, then each child would eventually achieve a normal, physical, personal and sexual maturity. He determined from a careful clinical scrutiny of the sex lives of his adult patients, as well as the observation of infants and the reports of their nursemaids, that though we have inborn biological drives and preset erogenous zones, the how and with whom we achieve our orgasms is concluded more by nurture than nature.

Freud taught that raising children to become sexually mature adults is an infinitely more complicated and challenging process, and must take into consideration the delicate complexities of nurture and nature in human sexual development and that severe personal and social conflicts can ensue when trauma or error occur during these times.

However disputed other elements of the Freudian literature may be, few can today seriously debate our debt to him for his germinal formulations on these dynamics of human sexuality. Imagine how provocative it must have been for his contemporary readers to hear that choice of partner and method of congress are cultural rather than strictly biological options for a satisfying sexual experience, and that the only inborn sexual elements are biological pressures for relief of sexual tension and erotic places on the body for climactic relief. Imagine how confused they would now be to learn that quantitatively superior, physiological climaxes are as often achieved when the object is self and the method is manual, as occurs with loved, liked or purchased partners, through conventional sexual methods. The fact is that by connecting the neurochemistry of our sexuality to the caring and kindness of others, we humans have the extraordinary capacity to enhance the existence of our species with interpersonal joy! On the other hand, when fear, confusion, depression and deprivation occur through developmentally noxious, interpersonal events, this alliance of sexual satisfaction and a joyous union is thwarted and perhaps eternally diminished. And it is on this issue that the sex-making and love-making distinction turns.

By investigating these variables in our interpersonal lives, we have a vital interest in knowing if our partner's intrinsic, biological potential for physical pleasure has been modified or distorted by cultural supports or contradictions. It is from such a scrutiny that we have come to understand such matters as why, despite a biological capability for on-going, repetitive sexual climaxes, many women have foresworn this physiological advantage in their here and now lives as retaliation against ancient hurts or why impotence and hostility characterize the sex lives of their male partners rather than tenderness and joyous relief. My best example of the complexity of the sexual nature versus nurture argument is that of a young patient of mine who wrote a one-act play about a lady with two vaginas, one for fornication, the other for making love. In the delightful aftermath of a mutually exciting and orgasmic sexual encounter, her partner first inquires playfully, "Did you come?" and when reassured, he then wonders "Which one?" With this second question, the post-coital relaxation converts to an agitated confrontation. The pleasure of a prior orgasm is transformed into an obsessive, hostile curiosity. He worries. Has he been duped and exploited? Convinced that he was "making love," he now worries that he was only "fornicating."

This misunderstanding between fornication and mature love surely has been overworked in the medical and lay literature. Yet, in its most simple rebuttal, can any of us be expected to have profound or enduring loving relationships with anywhere near the frequency of having satisfying sexual encounters? Of course not. However, this method for denying the fact is sadly effective, i.e., hind-placing the "love" word upon those relationships, i.e., "I must have loved him," they say, "or else I never would have done it." In other words, "unless I was in love, I never would have made love!" Sorry, wrong on both counts. Those are the same people who, on later occasions, protest "Of course I love him; why else would I suffer so? Why else would I put up with all this crap?"

Can any of them dare to hear this answer? "Because you have a bad habit to compulsively repeat pain. Because of your fear to face the mystery of aloneness, you rationalize your choice with platitudes." This formula that meaningfulness in relationships naturally follows intercourse or pain is a tragically and tenaciously common one.

Avoiding the pleasure principle was misconstrued by some to suggest these people like pain. But, this is not true at all. No one "likes" pain. The truth is that neurotic, psychological inertia holds some people faster to the familiar, though painful, than to the mystery of the unknown with its potential for pleasure. Why? Because of shame, guilt, and embarrassment, those three harpies of confused sentiment, those leaders of the neurotic band of psychological defense which proclaim "is" is better than "not is" or "might be."

These partners have been ensnared into a *folie à deux*, a love delusion that there is no one better for either of them. Do they honestly believe that God set up all those little dyads on Easter morning, and now they have this awesome responsibility to stay together? The answer appears to be "Yes." Once they get the other to reflexively say, "I love you," then they own their love delusion, as well. Therefore, they need never do anything again but ring the "I-thought-you-said-you-love-me" bell. Once so entrapped, as so many of you know, the door of your relationship to them, like a gigantic mitral valve, will only let more of you in, and none of you out, without rupture. For proof of this, just ask anyone in a neurotic relationship why they don't just separate. Three hours later he or she will still be answering your simple question with, "You just don't seem to understand, etc. etc. etc." With this book, at least you (and maybe they, too) will understand this: that which is not a fact cannot be a fact of love.

Another perversion of the love word was first described by the pioneer psychoanalyst Otto Fenichel. He stated "While falling in love is certainly no perversion, it is a perversion if the only possible 'sexual/loving' excitement that exists is the feeling of one's own insignificance as compared to the magnificence of the partner."

Fenichel went on to explain that the feeling that "I am small and the beloved is great" is reminiscent of the time when this was literally true—when the person was a child and was nurtured by an adult. However, those feelings of protection by another are not "love" when they occur in adults. It is "pathological dependency" when the partners are not complete unto themselves, but parts of a greater whole. These folks have never become complete individuals. They need union to be able to feel their own existence. Moreover, they frequently have neither a genuine interest in or an idea about the real personality of the partner, and they can all too easily develop this same adoration for different partners from one day to another.

These relationships thrive on an over-estimation of the partner and a participation in his/her "greatness." It is not a togetherness which ensues, but incorporation, and that is why separation is so devastating. "You can't leave me," they shriek, "you are part of me." This mistaking of sexual interest, or consummation, for love produces "love addicts," namely persons who have never become complete individuals and who, therefore, need union to be able to feel their own existence.

In his book *Knots*, R. D. Laing, an esteemed English psychiatrist, poeticized much of what we have been talking about here. He called these patterns of human bondage "knots, tangles, fangles, impasses, disjunctions, whirligogs and binds." For example:

> "Jack falls in love with Jill's image of Jack taking
> it to be himself.
> She must not die, because then he would lose himself.
> He is jealous in case anyone else's image is reflected
> in her mirror.
> Jill is a distorting mirror to herself.
> Jill has to distort herself to appear undistorted
> to herself.
>
> -
>
> She wants him to want her
> He wants her to want him
> To get him to want her
> she pretends she wants him
> To get her to want him –
> he pretends he wants her
> Jack wants
> Jill's want of Jack."

Whatever you may call these crazy connections, they are surely not love, and as soon as you know that, it will be easier, oh, so much easier to end these tangles, fangles, whirlygogs and binds and try real love in the real world. Literally hundreds of thousands of couples are entwined in such absurd, destructive duos.

Shackled by myth and distortion, those sick and sad connections thrive on a partner's fear of being alone. "I would rather have the noise of my partner's anger than the silence of my own uncertainty," they each protest separately or together.

In a 1940 essay, Walter Lippmann discussed another dimension of this problem, brought on by the new medical capability of separating procreation and sex by birth control. He pointed out that no prior technological advance had ever mandated us to so specifically reexamine the differences between sex and love than the now real and common occurrence of recreational or non-procreational sex.

In the simple world of intercourse, Lippmann explained, where babies are produced who need parents, devotion to this triangle could be taught to equal love, and not much psychiatric or philosophic commentary is needed. However, after the arrival of inexpensive birth control, additional guidance through this new era was needed.

An early attempt to do this was made by Philip Solomon in his article in a 1957 issue of the *New England Journal of Medicine*. He posed this question: "What happens to the boy and girl who fall in love?" He answered, "The girl regards him as the hero he has been wishing he were and, accepting her verdict, he adores her for it. She, in turn, sees in his eyes the girl she has been yearning to be. Each gladly adopts the other's view for her/himself. But what they love is the idealized version of themselves." This phenomenon he labeled "infatuation," and its three necessary pre-conditions are:

1. There must be an appreciable discrepancy between the actual self and the ideal self. (In fact, in societies where ambition and competition are minimal, infatuation is virtually unknown, whereas in highly-competitive, modern civilization, full of ever-increasing standards and future goals, romantic infatuation is common.)

2. The sense of reality must be vulnerable to being put in abeyance.

3. Each person must possess some attributes in reality that the other finds attractive. Otherwise, each could not value the judgment of, or identify with, the other.

By a mechanism no more complex than hyphenating the word "love" in these relationships to "child-love," the hazards of an adult wandering into that dangerous wonderland can be significantly diminished. Perhaps a familiar example of those hazards will clarify our point, such as what happens when the so-named "loved" person repudiates the love protest. Initial and normal feelings of loss, hurt and sadness soon convert to violence and rage. By primitive logic, "loving" entitles them to a reciprocal commitment. "I am not okay without you," echoes through their frightened brains, and the reflex response, "you will not be okay without me" emerges. "If I can't have you, no one can." "If I can't have you to love, I will have you to harm." The rest of this scenario often makes the next day's headlines, for this is the formula for most domestic violence.

So, while Charlie, the law student from Pittsburgh, can easily have sex with acquiescing Sally from Kansas City, it does not follow that either has the courage, stamina or talent for the enterprise of loving. While each may assert, "I like you very much," or "it feels wonderful to be with you," both should know that "adult-loving" is not the next semantic step in their sex and liking games.

We shall return to this point in Chapter 8 when we discuss what adult love really is, but first a few lessons on the nature and the techniques for overcoming some major impediments to love.

2

Bitching as Love's Nemesis

Let's face it, we're no angels and folks can provoke other folks to legitimately dislike them or be annoyed by them. If we are hostile, irreverent or uncouth, we invite legitimate disappointment and complaint. If we shouldn't have done what we did, if it was insensitive, it was hostile, then complaining about it is not bitching. Bitching is not such normal complaining. Bitching is not a valid response to stress, bitching is not mature, nor is bitching gender-limited or biased. Bitching in all its forms and transmutations is a neurotic process incorporating almost every major mechanism of psychological defense. It is theater of the absurd played in suburbia. As a neurotic process, the bitcher may utilize any one of a number of the major psychological mechanisms of defense.

Bitching is transference, a displacement or projection of ideas, feelings, wishes, fears and confusions. It is redirecting ancient hurts and unresolved conflict into the here and now. That's why a psychiatrist is the most informed person to teach you about it for that's his stock in trade. Bitching is neurosis in action! Psychiatric therapy is an enterprise in understanding our ancient emotional history and by so doing exposing the psychological mechanisms of defense which, in our immature years, we fabricated to enable us to deal with our primal fears and uncertainties. The more we know about them the less necessary is it for us to adhere to them. The more we see them in our bitching partners, the clearer it becomes to us how they are controlled by these mechanisms and therefore more in need of therapy than hugging or, for that matter, forgiving, and certainly not forbearing.

Be warned, however, that understanding bitching mechanisms does not change the person bitching. As a matter of fact such understanding or interpretation is more often resented as a hostile invasion of privacy than appreciated as a helpful intervention. Also remember that understanding is neither judging nor caring. When others implore you to understand them, they very often presume that such understanding is a precondition to your accepting or loving them. They must be warned that this is not the case, for understanding merely increases your interpersonal options and, after reading this book, your understanding may as often be a ticket out of a relationship as a reason for staying in one.

Bitching is persistent, neurotic scratching at the interface of a relationship. Bitching does not respond nor alter with good advice. The "hitched in bitching" have a long history of failing the good advice test and will not separate without surgery at the fusion line of their pathological connections. They also need convalescence for healing in the aftermath of their traumatic separation. Therefore, only those who can accept the temporary initial pains and possible post-operative complications, as trade-offs against the continuation of their self-destructive bitching lifestyle, are candidates for the unhitching from bitching procedure.

In their personal life in general and in their love life in particular, people are far more complex, dynamic and dangerous than would appear at first glance. What we first see in our relationships is only a thin impression of what people really are. Not only are people responding to and interacting on real issues, they are also defending themselves against anxiety. To that extent, we are less present with each other than with our defenses, thus producing superficial, non-productive relationships in which we may both be victims.

Explanations of the primary mechanisms of psychological defense will now be provided and their relationship to bitching will be carefully detailed. Since these processes of defense are the primary elements of psychoneurosis, it follows that bitching is a subset of neurotic thinking and behaving. The reader will then be shown that, while it is quite simple to recognize a defense, it is an extremely complicated psychiatric undertaking to alter one.

The concept of "neurosis" was originally a medical one, but it has developed a popular meaning. In the vernacular, a neurotic person is weird, peculiar, or sick but, more importantly, someone whose social responses are unpredictable, whose mood is labile and whose behavior is aberrant and perplexing. Just one layer below all the inappropriate behavior is the neurotic reason, which makes it appropriate as a defense against anxiety.

However, these mechanisms of psychological defense are not your friends, though they may serve briefly to avoid anxiety and conflict. They are rampantly present in everyday life and are a major characteristic of bitching relationships. Therefore, it is incumbent upon us to first learn how to identify them and secondly to learn how we can extricate ourselves from those bitching relationships in which they prevail.

Because intimacy is both dangerous and precious, we have every right to be defensive against invasion into our privacy, but normal apprehension is not neurotic defense and, while there can be joy in overcoming the former, there is tragedy in persisting with the latter.

Though with a little training it is extremely easy to recognize a defense, it is a quite complicated undertaking to alter one, and an arduous personal endeavor. Beware, then, of your enthusiasm for simple explanations or promises derived from inspiration, to effect change in your recalcitrant, difficult and bitching partner. Folks don't change that easily. These mechanisms are often bedrock, character traits and bode ill for your relationships with those who cherish them, despite their arguments of a willingness to change.

In the middle of such a bitching contest, the innocent players may often be heard to exclaim "Stop it, Jane or John. This is me, your husband/wife. I'm not your mother, boss, etc. etc. I didn't cut you off on the highway this morning, I didn't demand that you work late, I didn't do any of the things that you now have decided to hold me responsible for. I'm not your whipping post. Stop distorting, displacing, rationalizing, isolating, intellectualizing, etc. Stop defending yourself against your own anxiety and get real."

Now, actually, folks don't really talk like that, they say "Shut up, you're wrong. Leave me alone." They don't, nor should they be expected to, analyze the bitching process. But the fact is, that while we all do some of that stuff some of the time, our bitching partners do it most of the time. Most folks can tolerate some anxiety without such regressive maneuvers but bitchers can't, and so, as you all know so well, it doesn't take much to confuse them or, from their point of view, abuse them, so they can retaliate as if you were the one responsible for all their bad and unresolved yesterdays and, of course, for their present anxiety.

Insight into these behaviors was derived from the most essential element of psychodynamic Freudian psychiatry, i.e., that signs and symptoms of mental illness are also defensive solutions to graver and more serious problems. For example, when the early psychoanalysts first encountered the so-called hysterical motor paralyses, or less of sensation, they learned that, by hypnosis, the secret reasons for these maladies could be discovered and the normal functions would return as a result of this new understanding.

A modern-day example of this phenomenon in my practice occurred when a lady patient arrived at a local emergency room with a paralysis of her right leg from the hip down to her toes. Careful history of immediately preceding events revealed that on the prior evening, for the twentieth time, she was thoroughly embarrassed in public by her husband's excessive drinking. Later that same evening she had this terrifying moment of truth in the driveway to her home. She roused her husband who was passed out in the front seat and directed him to open the garage doors. Upon completion of this task, while wobbling to the door at the rear of the garage, he stood pathetic and flaccid directly in front of the beaming headlights, shadowed against the brick rear wall. While nothing drastic actually happened then, it didn't take a genius to realize that some very important things were happening subconsciously to this otherwise gentle and obedient lady. Sure enough, with reassuring supportive listening and the lubrication of free mental associations into her unconscious, we arrived at this fantasy and death wish. In one split second, she confided, her foot inadvertently jammed onto the accelerator pedal, could have provided a catharsis for years of repressed hostility against her husband, but she was controlled by another unconscious force.

Rather than directly expressing this hostile fantasy, guilt and shame rushed in to defend her against herself. Then came punishment, her own against herself. She would immobilize that leg so the instrument of her homicidal wish would be erased forever!

Alas, to what lengths won't we go to protect ourselves from ourselves, and what burdens and deprivations will we suffer to keep from knowing how humanly frail we really are? I am reminded of a Lenny Bruce sketch when he was talking about Jackie Kennedy's behavior in the few seconds following the assassination of her husband. While a Pollyanna press may have wondered whether she was leaping to protect her husband from further injury, as she climbed over him and out of the back seat of their limousine, Lenny knew better. She was trying to save her own ass he proclaimed. And why not? What's so bad about being scared and running away?

The point is that not only does our damn conscience harbor all manner of admonitions about what's right and wrong, it is also presided over by our ego ideal which says, "If we don't do as we were told, if we do not do our best, we're not OK; we're less than ourselves. We're bad, or mean, or selfish or whatever it takes to make us feel guilty, if we don't either do it their way, or if we haven't become the ideal person they encouraged us to be."

This chapter is designed to first reveal these phenomena and then to suggest some remedies. After simple explanations of the primary mechanisms of psychological defense are provided, it will then be apparent that bitching is just another name for these mechanisms. And, since these processes of defense are the primary elements of psychoneurosis, it follows that bitching is a subset of neurotic thinking and behaving. The reader will then be shown that, while it is quite simple to recognize a defense, it is an extremely complicated psychiatric undertaking to alter one.

Beware then of your enthusiasm for simple explanations, or promises derived from inspiration, to effect change in your recalcitrant, difficult and bitching partner. Folks don't change that easily. These mechanisms are often bedrock character traits and bode ill for your relationships with those who cherish them, despite their promises to change.

Despite his arguments and pleadings to the contrary, our bitching partner's need to protect himself from his own unconscious rage, fear, sexual or aggressive impulses, is much more important than concessions to the reality of your needs. Should they erupt as a result of your depriving him of his defensive maneuver, you are both in for a substantially more dangerous confrontation.

The first studied mechanisms to control this fearsome anxiety, as we noted earlier, were repression and conversion. Repression was defined as "the automatic and seemingly effortless, involuntary relegation of consciously repugnant or intolerable ideas, feelings, wishes, motives, beliefs and impulses into non-awareness." Somatic conversion, as in the paralysis of the lower extremity of my patient, is "the unconscious expression by our bodies of these same repressed feelings."

The body itself may speak with any of its systems—ulcer, asthma, high blood pressure, muscle paralysis, sensorial deficiencies, etc.

These somatic processes were also known to the ancient Greeks who called them "hysteria." Their view was that the uterus was loosened from its moorings in the pelvis and was wandering in the body, adversely affecting whatever other organ it happened upon. They were wrong in believing that the disease was exclusively one in women, but they were right to appreciate that unfulfilled, unsatisfied or forbidden sexual wishes, symbolized by the wandering uterus, was the root cause of the symptoms of anxiety, with its accompanying physical weaknesses and somatic conversions.

This ancient Greek notion of repressed ideas and feelings, causing symptoms, was most-creatively expanded and popularized by Sigmund Freud who, in turn, based his work on the teachings of two contemporary French researchers, Janet and Charcot, who had postulated that "fixed ideas" locked in the subconscious recesses of the mind could (1) be released by the medical hypnosis. The techniques were then called animal magnetism, first described by Anton Mesmer, and (2) could be implanted into the unconscious mind of a subject which would then compel him to behave in a certain fashion without his conscious control or understanding.

A superb example of this was reported by Freud himself, recounting a demonstration by Charcot, where a beleaguered and confused subject was trying to explain or rationalize why he had, in a post-hypnotic state, opened his umbrella in a lecture hall at a most inopportune time, in a most inappropriate manner. All the members of the audience knew that this behavior was responsive to a key word spoken by the lecturer during the induction phase of his subject's hypnosis, but only Freud realized that, while the route of ingress of such ideas was hypnosis, the route of egress of such ideas need not be hypnosis, but could be free, unfettered mental associations.

In one small moment in the life of a hapless student, in a French medical classroom, one gigantic leap for mankind was taken in the form of Freud's insightful genius. Alas, he postulated, if a prehypnotic suggestion can be extricated from the mind of a hypnotized subject by free mental associations, then perhaps all ideas and feelings, hiding in the recesses of the unconscious, not just those placed by hypnosis, can be thus extricated. With such a catharsis of hidden repressed ideas, he further hypothesized that signs and symptoms of mental illness could then be relieved. Thus was psychoanalysis born.

A little known, coincidental fact is that Mary Baker Eddy, the founder of Christian Science, was herself also a believer in Anton Mesmer's theory of animal magnetism and likewise much of her whole enterprise of faith healing was derived from these same hypotheses, namely that faith in or understanding of the power of mind could tremendously alter its effect on the body. She, of course, did not limit her theory to such belief relieving only mental illness, but applied it to all illnesses of the body.

Subsequent elaboration of these ideas, over the next half-century, by Freud himself and his students, established these ancillary facts to be true, namely that life experiences were deposited in two major vaults of the brain, one for facts, the other for the associated feelings generated by those facts. Consider now that while the facts go promptly into storage, there is a lag phase where the emotions generated by those facts may be dissipated or expressed and, thus, not stored or deposited with the same volume or intensity with which they arrived.

Furthermore, when those feelings are repressed, they do not lie dormant in their vaults of repression, but exert their presence in extremely creative and devious ways. They emerge by fashioning compromises between what is true and what can be tolerated. They produce one or another of the many neurotic mechanisms of psychological defense. They insinuate themselves deep into the character structure of those who are forced to utilize them and who thusly have to fake their true identity.

Perhaps this example will clarify these past several points: Mrs. W.'s childhood was fraught with events and experiences of deprivation and abuse, beginning with the desertion of her natural father, and culminating in her placement in foster care, due to her mother's alcoholism. In her adult life, she denied those facts by repressing the anger, depression and rage which they engendered. Yet, in her present marriage, she harvests those feelings and directs them against her mother-in-law by forbidding her children to see their paternal grandparents, because of "their stupid politics." Mrs. W. is also cold and frigid to her husband whenever he reminisces with their daughter about his happy childhood.

Now it doesn't take a training analyst at a big city institute of psychoanalysis with twenty years on the couch himself to figure out what's going on. (1) She is displacing onto an innocent mother-in-law, for spurious reasons, her repressed hostility against her own rejecting mother; (2) She is seeding the destruction of her own marriage and the not unlikely loss of custody of her child, by projecting her husband into her negative prophecy that all men leave women, and their children are then taken away. She has identified with her deserting mother. These whats and whys of her behavior and emotion are actually simple to comprehend.

The "how to stop it" is a formidable task. Freud oversimplified the answer with this simple aphorism of therapy, "Where id was there shall ego be." He did not say, "Where stupid was, there shall intelligence be," or "Where wrong information was, there shall right information be." What he said was, "Where good advice fails, psychotherapy begins."

While not as severe as the primary, process thinking of the psychotic, such as delusions and hallucinations, neurotic mechanisms of defense borrow from that same library of failing-to-test reality. If I have hateful feelings for my mother for abandoning me in my childhood, then I can hate your mother for burning the toast, because they are both mothers, aren't they? And she did burn the toast, didn't she? This is bedrock bitching. This is dangerous stuff. You don't get better from this with a hug!

A more dramatic expression of this phenomenon is expressed in the newspaper headline which reads "18-Year-Old Man Rapes an 80-Year-Old Woman." Clearly no adolescent rapes an 80-year-old woman for sexual pleasure! Rage and hate have been sexualized, real objects of today have been substituted for yesterday's villains. While bitching is seldom the equivalent of such a gross example of displaced sexual and aggressive emotions, neither are easily remedied.

The path to resolution of such distortions and displacements is arduously long. In most instances, the defenses imbed themselves into the person's personality and, as one author commented, become his character armor.

Perhaps another example will clarify this. Fred was a handsome, well-traveled entrepreneur in a small, New England, fishing town. His wife had a university appointment in a local junior college history department. After nine years of marriage, a manifest complaint of his drinking and drunken behavior led to separation and a suit for divorce. A last-ditch enterprise to save their union occurred when he decided to enroll in an alcohol treatment program. Twenty-eight days later, sober with one AA chip, he was ready to live happily ever after because, as he said, "I won't do what I did before—drink and get drunk." He would modify his drinking behavior. But will he modify his character, or does he still distort, displace, deny and measure others by the same ruler of defensive prejudice?

Three marriage counseling sessions into his convalescence, we get closer to the answer to these questions.

She to him:

So my assignment in therapy is:

1. Forgive the humiliation of your drunken infidelities, to a person known to both our families.

2. Forget the rantings of "whore" and "pig" which echoed along the corridors to our eight-year-old daughter's bedroom.

3. Forbear the pushing and shoving and the walkouts and never knowing if or when you will be back.

And your task is:

1. Learn to be less critical of my cooking and housekeeping which, even without alcohol, seems to still annoy the hell out of you!

"Could it be, Fred," she finally blurts out, "that you just don't like me or the woman I have become since I went back to school and got my teaching assistant-ship?"

Seizing this opportunity for bringing to their discourse the muse of reason, he replies, "Is it not reasonable for me to expect that you direct the maid to mop behind the couch?"

To which she retorts, "And is it not reasonable for me to expect you to know and care about how vulnerable I am to any and all reminders of how it was, when such a complaint was overture to an opera of profanity and abuse?"

"You just don't like women!" she exclaims. "And you're afraid of intimacy."

Well, maybe she's right and maybe not, but if she is right, he can't fix this estrangement by not drinking anymore, because it is "bone of his bone," it is embedded in his character. But, most importantly, it began as a defensive mechanism. It began as a solution to the problems of fear of abandonment, and the terror of losing himself in the act of giving. But he was not that way in the new-born nursery. He had to have become that way, and the process often involves several major, mental mechanisms of psychological defense which were required to avoid anxiety, panic and the terror of abandonment. If a child's desire for intimacy was too often frustrated by failures in his developmental years, then, like an experimental rat in a psychological maze, his survival requires finding another route to the corn.

Symptoms and signs of mental illness and psychological mechanisms of defense represent these other routes to the corn and are better solutions than the raw panic and anxiety which would occur without them. That's why these partners don't just change, they are not bitching at your personal existence, but at your presence—the catalyst for their anxiety.

It's not that Fred doesn't like Mary because she doesn't know how to make lasagna, or she has become too educated. It's because he's afraid of what she has found in him, his fears of adequacy, his anxiety about his work. And once again, you don't fix that by a hug! And it doesn't happen only to the Freds of the world, it happens to the Joans and the Janes and the Juliets. How many guys or gals do you know who just can't win for losing in their marriages? Absolutely nothing that they do is right. "Don't touch me; leave me alone," their wives or husbands protest. It's not that they can't be handled, but that they can't handle it. I'm too afraid. I'm too fragile. I'm too insecure. I'm too frightened to dare to try and fail again, to dare to surrender and, if abandoned, have to start all over. At least when I stay the way I am, I exist."

So why did they get into these relationships in the first place? Answer: With the fantasy that what was, was not true. Wish prevailed over truth, rationalization prevailed over reason, to produce another shoot-out at the "I'm Not OK Corral."

The fat lady has begun to sing at last when we identify this bedrock issue of most bitching relationships, namely where mechanisms of defense have converted to issues of character, and where values, which are derived from these mechanisms, are converted to character armor which cannot be penetrated by love and caring. Reason is beaten by rationalization in each round of their encounter. Our defensive partners are not stupid, they are most often quite bright. Yet they argue their positions with a relentless zeal, as if their lives depended upon it and, what we soon learn is that, their emotional lives very often do depend upon it.

Perhaps this additional example of several of these processes in a lady patient of mine, will clarify this point.

Tearful and embarrassed, to the point of almost catatonia, Mrs. K. was driven to my office by her attorney's secretary. All the attorney said in the call which preceded her arrival was, "You've got to help me with this one, today, Alfred."

What happened was that Mrs. K., a recently widowed 54-year-old lady and retiree, after thirty years at a large, New England food processing company, was picked up for shoplifting a hose spigot from a discount store. With fear and trembling, Mrs. K. related that despite the fact she and her sister, Margaret, had planned a beach outing that Saturday morning, Margaret had gone without her. As if that wasn't bad enough, earlier that month, the same sister, also a widowed lady, met a gentleman from Pittsburgh and, what began as a mutual admiration for the quarterbacking of Terry Bradshaw and the fancy skating of Mario Lemieux, was slowly converting into plans for a fall wedding.

Well, I can tell you that Mrs. K. was damn mad. "Do you realize," she protested, "that hardly once in all her visits did Margaret ever think to pick up a check at even a Wendy's? Do you know," she went on, "that when Margaret pops Mrs. K.'s corn in the microwave, she only rarely asks, 'Oh, by the way, Mary, would you like some?' Sometimes I would just like to tell her off," Mary said. "I could just punch her," she blurted out, followed by a psychological melt-down of the following childhood memories.

Margaret was Mary's younger sister by five years and, though only a child herself, it was Mary who cuddled and calmed and fed her, during those emotional days when their mother, sick with what the doctors called post-partum depression, would just sit and stare at the dirty clothes piling up on the bedroom floor, or at the empty refrigerator.

"It's up to you, Mary," her anguished father would say when he left for twelve- to fourteen-hour factory days, "to see that Margaret is well taken care of." Chronic disability soon set in for Mary's mother with many, many, state hospitalizations (one for almost eighteen months), in the days of regressive shock therapy and high doses of mummifying drugs.

Long hours of babysitting, no money for high school proms or college, led to festering and progressive resentments in Mary, if not death wishes against the innocent sister herself, a victim of the same, fated deprivations.

"Sometimes I wish she just hadn't been born," this pro-lifer blurted. However, for these forbidden wishes, her strict Catholicism demanded that someone had to pay. So now, thirty years later, in a manifest mood of anger and disappointment about not going to the beach, the ancient hate erupted. However, she must be punished for these thoughts, and so, of course, she was. Handcuffed and fingerprinted at a busy county jail, with new felons and recidivists, she sat in a cold cell until the "Release on Her Own Recognizance" people came to let her go with a sheaf of papers which began: "The State vs. Mrs. K., Case #2236488." The power of the unconscious once again prevailed over reason and propriety.

Who, after fifty years of post-Freudian literature, can deny its ominous and ubiquitous presence? What goes around, comes around; what goes in will eventually come out. Mrs. K.'s crime will not make the headlines, but its psychodynamics are clear, turning against the self with a mixture of displacement and distortion, a cacophony of mental mechanisms at work, the bedrock of self-destructive relationships.

Yes, they too had a bitching relationship, insofar as it was characterized by fear, denial and distortion and, while not husband and wife, or boyfriend and girlfriend, the issues were the same—two people striving for intimacy and thwarted by several mental mechanisms of defense and repressed old angers and frustrations.

In our next chapter I shall elaborate upon this theme, with a more precise explanation of the major mechanisms of defense most often associated with the bitching process.

3

The Psychodynamics of the Nine
Major Mechanisms of Psychological Defense

The primary psychodynamics of these major mechanisms of defense were, as we mentioned in the previous chapter, first propounded by Freud himself in some of his earliest papers. However, they were given their most definitive presentation by his daughter, Anna, some thirty years later and have remained the bedrock concept of almost all current personality theories. As we mentioned in Chapter 1, these early analysts noted that the "manifest content" of their patients' conversations and behavior was usually quite different from what they really meant to convey and, more precisely, only what they could tolerate to share. The "latent content," or hidden meanings, were soon discovered to be too dangerous or shameful to express and, therefore, could only be discovered by undoing the processes which concealed them in the first place. The generic name of this concealment was called "repression," and in every standard textbook of psychology and psychiatry, its many variations are listed as the psychological mechanisms of defense.

In this chapter, I shall elaborate upon the nine most importantly and frequently used mechanisms of bitching relationships, i.e., (1) projection, (2) idealization with introjection, (3) displacement, (4) reaction formation, (5) identification, (6) rationalization/intellectualization, (7) turning against the self, (8) phobia, and (9), somatization.

Each of these mechanisms achieves a safer world, for the person who uses them, than would be possible without such a maneuver. Those who confront such a person with the reply "Get real!" or "Get a life!" are right on target with their intuitive awareness that such folks, for reasons which they themselves do not understand, cannot tolerate their lives without certain defensive alterations but, more importantly, produce behaviors, attitudes and ideas which are intolerable to us, i.e., bitching!

Projection

For some, projection is the prototype of all mental mechanisms of defense and the Schreber case is the classic example of this.

Against the advice of friends, Daniel Paul Schreber, a German Appeals Court Judge of superior mental gifts and unusual keenness of intellect, decided "to close my eyes to the difficulties which would appear to lie in the path of publication ... so that qualified authorities could hold some inquiry into my personal experience." Thus, in 1903, his autobiography, *Memoirs of a Nerve Patient*, was published.

Taking him at his word, eight years later, Sigmund Freud published his analysis of Schreber's autobiography, *The Schreber Case*, providing a classic elucidation of the defense mechanisms underlying paranoid thinking, in general, and pathological jealousy, in particular.

Freud's definition of "projection" provided classic insight into all defense mechanisms, i.e., "An internal perception is suppressed and its content, after undergoing a certain kind of distortion, enters consciousness in the form of an external perception. Thus, I see not what is without, but what is within, projected upon what is without."

As with all mechanisms of defense, projection operates outside of conscious awareness. Unacceptable aspects of the self are rejected and disowned. They are then thrown outward, projected upon others. The projector then reacts and responds, as if the projects belonged to the innocent others.

The person does not do it with a cognitive purpose, he is not aware that he or she is doing it, and will deny that it is so if confronted with your conclusions that it is.

When understanding the projective mechanism, we learn that the apparent behavior, or feelings, of others may be our own projections upon them, as a defense against the anxiety which would otherwise beset us in the real and undefended world.

For example, Paul says he loves Mary, and Mary believes him. The problem is that he doesn't trust her. He doesn't trust the way she walks, talks or moves. He worries about what she is thinking or feeling, and he believes most other folks have nothing better to do than desire her. He worries about what her real, sexual feelings are and thinks everybody wants her and that she does not properly resist their sexual wishes. He also always wants to know where she is and what she is doing. He wants to know why she is looking at what she is looking at, and is quick to anger and become belligerent when he thinks someone else is looking at her. He is malignantly jealous, and the mechanism of malignant jealousy is a reconstruction of the simple elements of projection, as follows:

The fact is Paul has infidelity in his heart. He spends much time crusading against illicit sex and in favor of purity of soul. He worries about people who slow dance and thinks all those pelvic gyrations are obscene. He watches the book list at the local grade school to see that no allusions to adultery are included. Because he cannot dare to probe into his own unconscious, he projects his feelings first upon random strangers and then upon Mary herself.

Further analysis of such fellows as Paul has also noted that they are almost universally homophobic, and that one level below that defensive maneuver is an even more sinister, hidden agenda. What they have observed lurking in the nether places of their unconscious are these even more forbidden wishes, i.e., "I have homosexual desires for those same men." However, because this is too intolerable for them to bear, they conclude that those persons desire them and that's why they are staring at him so furtively. They then go on to fantasize: "Well, if he doesn't stop, I'll fix him with a punch in the face, because I'm no fag. As a matter of fact, I hate fags and I suppose fags hate me. That's why he's trying to get me, he wants to hurt me!"

However, whether it's hating gay men or pathological jealousy, it turns out that on more careful scrutiny, it's all just another example of how a neurotic defense mechanism produces bitching, and produces unhappy relationships.

Idealization and Introjection

Idealization and introjection are often described together because of their close connection to the psychodynamics of depression. Here an object or person is emotionally over-rated, not in accord with real attributes but with the needs of the observer.

For example, even in public places, before total strangers, Sarah would destroy Herman with looks or remarks and, on occasion, with not-so-loving punches on his shoulder or back. "He's so stupid," she said on a regular basis, when she learned he forgave an enemy or showed affection to one of his employees. Herman, on the other hand, would not only take it, but worshipped Sarah. She could do no wrong; she was his Sarah, and God forbid that anyone dare to speak unkindly of her.

After years of these deeply conflicted—if not tormented years—with his spouse, Herman was at last spared. Complications of diabetes took Sarah to her final rest, while Herman, a still young and healthy 64-year-old, had perhaps another decade or two to be himself. Some who knew them, admired his tolerance and acceptance of her belligerence. Others wondered why he just didn't slap her down or leave. But everyone who was ever with them saw her as a virago and him as the wimp of their relationship, even though he was otherwise a successful businessman. So now that she's dead, will he allow himself a normal grief period and then go on with his life? Absolutely not! He wears black to work, eats very little, seldom goes out with friends, and is often noted to be rocking or crying on his office sofa. What's going on here? Answer: introjection. Sarah lives in Herman, still protected from his anger against her, expressed as depression. How do we know this? Answer: from the thousands of Hermans whose psychotherapy reveals this to be so. "I was very angry with you when you were alive which I could not express, and I am furious with you now for leaving me, before I could express it."

When the hostility toward the introject reaches its peak, the depression can turn to suicide which is really killing the person within.

Displacement

Displacement is a mechanism by which an emotional feeling is transferred from its internal location to an external object.

Sally had, while growing up, a contradictory and confusing relationship with her alcoholic father. As a preteenager, when she was asexual and adorable, he would, whether sober or drunk, over-cuddle and spoil her. She was Daddy's little girl and his frequent touching of her was considered OK. However, when she began to fill out, his attitude became radically different. Strict discipline and mean remarks would frequently send her to her room in tears. His epithets about promiscuity and out-of-wedlock pregnancies were demeaning and belligerent.

Now, ten years later, she is a frigid and frightened young mother who cannot stand to be touched by a loving and sensitive husband. Since the beginning of their marriage, he couldn't win for losing. "Why are you treating me this way?" he would incredulously inquire.

Only in brief moments, of short-lived expressions of remorse, could she say, "It's not you, David, it goes back a long time." And surely it did! A trapped, attractive young woman, still trying to untangle herself from a relationship to a troubled father whose emotional immaturity about his daughter is now revealed one generation later in her sexual frigidity, in the form of the displacement of her anger with her father onto her husband.

Reaction Formation

A primary example of this frequent mechanism is "love expressed as hate," or "wish expressed as repudiation." A child who has been disappointed, or mistreated by a parent, may invert the feelings of retaliation to become an adult who is zealously overindulgent and overprotective of that parent. Such a caretaker daughter, suffering from reaction formation, may behave as a most indulgent individual, only to be revealed in psychoanalysis as harboring unbearable death wishes against the same parent.

Another, commonly cited manifestation of this defense is the zealous protagonist of prohibition who has inverted his real desire to drink alcohol.

Mary also provides an excellent example of both reaction formation and introjection. Not only was her father a physically dangerous man with his strong, broad frame, but his unpredictability was even more serious. If she looked pretty, he admonished her for being too seductive or, if she was unkempt, he would call her a slob or trashy. The way he treated her mother was his most despicable trait. With or without alcohol, he would refer to her as "Bitch" or "Woman" and, though only half his size, she would frequently have to physically defend herself with slaps and scratching to avoid his fists and heels. The image of him going into their bedroom with her mother cowering in the corner, still gives Mary goosebumps.

So please explain why, since his death in an industrial accident, has Mary become so forlorn and withdrawn? She's hardly left her room since the funeral and refuses to talk about it. The others at home can hear her pacing at all hours of the night, and she never comes to the table for meals and only occasionally is seen snacking on crackers and iced tea. It looks as if someone has placed a terrible curse on her. Her husband, Jason, said it's almost as if she were possessed by a terrible secret.

Three months of therapy later, the secret is no longer lodged under the weight of guilt. Mary can now see that she "incorporated" her father into her inner-self and then converted, by reaction formation, her hostility against him, against that same inner-self, in the form of an unremitting depression.

Identification

When one becomes more like another than himself, it is called identification. The process may be positive if the other is admired, but is often, by paradox, negative when the identification is with someone who is disliked or feared. The latter situation is called "identification with the aggressor." For example, while consciously disliking certain traits of their parents, many offspring are unconsciously drawn to mime them in their adult lives. Because nurture, like nature, abhors a vacuum, we can't grow up to be a "not someone." We will, for better or for worse, identify with those who model for us during our formative years. Excellent evidence of this can be found in children of alcoholic parents who, while manifestly despising them, often become very much like them. Another example of "identification with the aggressor" is the child pretending to be a ghost and scaring his playmates, as a mechanism of warding off his own personal fears. This is also easily discerned in a child playing doctor or dentist, trying to ward off their apprehension about the next visit, by being the doctor himself.

Rationalization/Intellectualization

These defenses are not the province of the intelligentsia, for they imply no special talent of their users, since the process, as in all defenses, is unconscious. In this instance, the unconscious uses the intellect or reason as its servant to allay anxiety while distorting reality. The bedrock of this mechanism is simply this:

There are many rational reasons why an event may have occurred, but only one may be correct or true. The everyday examples of this go from the absurd and ridiculous to the bizarre and fantastic. Yet, in each, the reason is logical and makes sense. It's just wrong.

Take a look at these several marriages and you will see what I mean. Husband, Charles, comes home from work late almost every day of the workweek. "You wouldn't want me to lose my job?" he exclaims, when his wife, Jane, asks for a little more help with the children and a reliable plan for serving the evening meal. The fact is his boss often tells him to go home early and let some of the late day's work go to tomorrow. But Charlie is fed up with his domestic scene and won't admit that avoiding his marriage is what all that overtime is about.

Now that the children are grown and she and her husband, Lenny, can at last travel together for holidays and his business trips, Barbara has figured out that visiting her ailing mother in a nursing home, twice a week, is a must, in order for her to fulfill her filial responsibilities. "Suppose something happens while we are away?" she protests, "I'd never forgive myself."

Clearly Barbara and Charles have said something quite reasonable, but patently false. They have used reason not in the pursuit of the resolution of marital discord, but to conceal their own limitations and fears. A second fact is that they do this unconsciously, without themselves realizing what they are doing. If they did, it would not be rationalization, it would be outright deceit and manipulation. And, of course, that is why it is so difficult to remedy.

Example #3: Since her first day in elementary school, until their therapy session, three years later, Ted and Cindy have been at each other's throat about how to discipline their daughter, Liana. The tension is so thick in their home, you can cut it with a knife. If they make love once every two months, it's a lot, and neither of them still calls it lovemaking. Ted explains it easily! The tension between Cindy and Liana turns him off. We can all agree that's a very good reason, but is it the correct one? In private therapy sessions, Cindy confides that anyone who knows Ted will testify he would rather be with his computer than a real live girl. It's only Ted who doesn't know.

Turning Against the Self

The mechanism known as "Turning Against the Self" often underlies what is generally referred to as "masochism." It is more often seen in our culture among women than men. The scenario begins with the child establishing an attitude against the parents for an often-arbitrary set of their faults. Early on the reactive emotion of anger may be released in the little girl's naughtiness or general unruliness. However, if this energy is released too vehemently, the child fears she will be punished or abandoned. She may therefore turn this hostility against herself, in unjustified self-accusations and feelings of unworthiness. Such personal suffering neutralizes her aggression against her parents. Using this mechanism accounts not only for the continuation of poor marriages in later life, but staying in poor jobs and overall staying in many other poor, personal relationships.

For example, Mabel's marriage to Richard was classic for the wife of an alcoholic husband. But this time, not below the poverty level, but many rungs above it. Richard held a very important sales position with a manufacturer of women's clothing. "The rag business" as he called it, required, or so he persuaded her, entertaining buyers with "anything they wanted—booze, women and, of course, a piece of the action." Mabel said, "It would have been all right if it was just that he had a few girlfriends out of town, or that he missed almost every occasion of significance in the lives of his three daughters—first communion, graduation and not even one hospital visit while their youngest, Louise, had double pneumonia. Demeaning Mabel in public, her weight, her dowdiness, her prudishness, was par for the course and had become just part of the way they lived. Not making any effort to conceal an extended affair, begun with the teenage sister of one of the maintenance men at the factory, still didn't excite Mabel to rebel and take some action to assert "I don't deserve this disrespect and I won't take it anymore."

Mabel by now had a substantial stock interest in Richard's company and the house was in her name, also. Why didn't she leave? The girls were grown. It's not as if she didn't have a circle of supportive lady friends. "Let me explain it to you this way, Dr. Fireman" she said one day. "When Richard and I met, we both had nothing. In my parents' house, we girls were nothing. My two brothers went to college and no one noted whether I did or didn't go to high school, let alone graduate. From the time I was old enough to reach the sink, I was doing dishes, washing clothes, making lunches for my two younger brothers and babysitting while my mother did the same for some other lady down the street."

"Don't ask," mother would say, "and you won't be disappointed."

In fact, Mabel never did ask for much, but more importantly never felt she deserved much either: "Richard was not evil. It's just that he soon learned with me, he could get away with anything and the more he got away with, the less he cared or respected me."

Phobia

Phobias are examples of several mechanisms of psychological defense coalescing into a symptom of mental illness. The phobia of animals, heights or the marketplace represents distortions, displacements and projections of our hidden fears, upon objects which, in reality, are quite neutral and benign. By further rationalization, however, these fears are explained away with platitudes.

Take the case of a person phobic of elevators. While it may not be totally inappropriate to tense up when boarding an elevator, when a person prefers to climb twelve flights of stairs rather than endure a closed space, that is an irrational defense against something else. Considering psychological mechanisms of defense, however, we are able to understand this phobia. While there is some rationale for being concerned within the closed space of an elevator, vis-à-vis its mechanical efficiency or reliability, when we expand our thinking by one orbit into psychological defenses, an explanation for the "irrational" panic which besets our phobic patient is soon found. In a setting where flight to a neutral space is physically prohibited, the ability to avoid acting-out dangerous feelings, or wishes, in his mind, is dangerously compromised. It is not that the elevator will come crashing to the ground from a broken cable (which would be "fear" rather than "phobia"—an important difference), but that repressed feelings will rage and soar higher and faster than the elevator, in an environment where escape to a neutral zone is emphatically compromised.

Perhaps other examples will make the point a bit clearer.

Little Johnny is what we psychiatrists call "school phobic." That is to say, he is manifestly afraid to go to school, but, in fact, that is not what he is afraid of. He is afraid of leaving his mother, for if *his* mother were to go to school with him, he would be fine. On the days that he does go to school, he rushes home as fast as he can, and is manifestly relieved when he sees her smiling face. His recurring fantasy, which he confided to his therapist, is that, while at school, *his* house will burn down. His manifest phobic complaint insulates him, at least for now, from coming to terms with *his* latent fears of being abandoned by his mother. No effort to make school an easy place will remedy this problem. The problem is his insecurity about leaving his home.

Thirty-five-year-old Eric had his first panic attack while crossing the Skyway Bridge from St. Petersburg to Bradenton, Florida. He now takes the inland route (ten miles further) to commute between his home on one side of Tampa Bay and his job on the other side, because he is "afraid of bridges." However, Eric is afraid of having another panic attack and, in his mind, they are had on bridges.

While these phobias are not conspicuously present in bitching relationships, I cite them as opportunities in which the mechanisms of displacement and distortion contort a person's ability to face, realistically, more important and underlying issues that beset them in their enterprise of being personally, vocationally and socially successful.

In an early paper of mine, I coined the term "recreation phobia" and would like to insert some discussion of it here, in the aftermath of these several paragraphs, to show how pandemic the phobic problem is and how it occurs in places that we sometimes least expect. I began my paper by talking about "success phobia" where people frequently fall ill when a deep-rooted, long-cherished, but conflicted, wish has come to fulfillment or approaches that hour. I then proceeded to show how, in recreational phobia, several, similar, unconscious factors which occur in "classic success phobia," are also present in recreational phobia.

I demonstrated how an overdeveloped and neurotic work ethic creates the sin of playing. For, if to work is divine, then to not work fulfills the devil's plan of finding his work for idle hands. Underlying this phobia is a vulnerability to the shame of exposure, ridicule and laughter for not playing well, being awkward or limited in one's play skills. I then asked these two questions: (1) Where did we get this crazy idea that how we ski down a mountain, dance a jig, or frolic in a wading pool puts our self-worth in jeopardy? and (2) How can we get rid of it?

Whether we call it "stage fright" or "paranoia," this sad over-investment in the hazard of being observed by others—in our less controlled, free, more playful and creative moments—represents a real problem for couples. While this particular defense may not be found in a standard text of psychiatry, it plays a major role in bitching relationships and is worth further study.

Free-time provides both "play time" and "time to know that we don't know how to play." We are recognized at work as doctor, secretary, plumber or judge, and the terms of our social contract are set. But "player" invites us to renew the innocence and vulnerability of our childhood. When you give up the familiarity and the ritual of the work role, you move a few steps closer to the repressed. Somehow, as a child, you got into your most embarrassing and punishable situations while at play. I'm sure you can remember some excruciating moments. But that was then, not now—or is it?

One marriage counselor tried to fashion a therapy program based on this issue, by having troubled couples come into a playroom in his office. Whether it was "Monopoly," or electric trains with trestles and bridges that had to be opened and closed by a prearranged and coordinated effort, the counselor frequently found, by watching his clients play these games, that there was "playing trouble" in a couple's marriage. He detected a unique limitation in either of their abilities to "play." On the basis of his work, he wrote a whole new chorale on the bitching of sore-losers and arrogant winners and play-phobic-abstainers.

His point, which I hope this chapter enhances, was that you should take a careful reading of what sort of "player" you have in the life game of your relationships, and be wary of the person who says, "Don't you dare call our relationship a game!" He is the same one who has no place for laughter and humor in relationships, and is so stuck in the sandbox of yesterdays that he really cannot be cast as a reliable player in your present life.

Psychosomatization

Since Johnny's first absence from school because of a fever or a hacking cough, to the favors accorded adolescent girls at "that time of the month," to mother's withdrawal from sexual availability because of a "headache," medical illness has been used and abused as a reliable and efficient excuse from any personal or vocational tasks which the individual considers noxious or painful. "Not feeling well" can always provide at least temporary respite from undesirable social activities. "I'm sick! Can't you see I'm sick?" This protest not only has secured the defense of "not guilty by reason of insanity," which expiates the defendant from criminal responsibility, it also has been used to avoid the assignments and responsibilities which would otherwise be expected from a well body.

In psychosomatization reactions, I am talking about the abused social and situational advantages of physical illness, I am not referring to the proper rights of medically-ill patients to receive generous and humane care and pardon from tasks otherwise expected from them when they are healthy.

Medical students are scarcely into their first clinical year when they realize that a high percentage of the physical complaints of their patients are psychologically determined. They also soon learn about the serious problems of secondary, psychological advantage even when "real" illness does occur. It takes only one or two afternoons in the office of a general practitioner to reveal that such functional, physical complaints as diarrhea, nausea, headache or fatigue are as often the body's language of revealing fear, disappointment, depression, confusion or conflict, as they are messages of pathological processes from diseased organs.

The body is not limited to speech and gesture for its communication. The pale look of the infirm body is as persuasive as poetic, verbal pleading. Few patients, however, say, "I know these body complaints are my defensive conversions to psychophysiological reactions, because of underlying psychological problems." Quite to the contrary, they insist on their legitimacy! "Can't you see I'm sick?" they ask with undiminished zeal, despite unsuccessful, medical efforts to find the causes of their complaints.

It is a standard joke on the internal medicine floors and outpatient departments that "When the chart weighs five pounds, it's time for a psychiatric consult." We psychiatric residents, unfortunately, also knew there were few limits of procedures or surgeries that patients would not first endure before they would consider there was a mind-over-body factor which contributed to, if not caused, their illness.

It was not so much, we residents in both specialties soon learned, that the patients wanted to be cured, as that the patients wanted to be touched. The transition from the touching probes of surgical and diagnostic instruments, to the listening ears of a caring psychiatrist, often proves arduously complex for this tragically simple reason. Folks are more terrified to confront their loneliness and the hazard of being unlovable than the pain of operative procedures. The symbolic "caring" that these procedures convey is more reliable for them than the chance that, if the true issues are revealed, no one will heed their call.

Those connected to the complainers, by marriage or other circumstances, have a deep suspicion that these psychosomatic, or conversion traits, represent an unconscious forfeiture of conventional language, in favor of physical language, as the proper mechanism for resolving interpersonal problems. The inevitable stresses of the relationships on the complainers is all too frequently punctuated by the time-out times in which they are "too sick to talk."

A careful, psychoanalytical investigation of such complaints often reveals them to be neurotic conversions of "yesterday's old business" into today's asthmatic attack, diarrhea, menstrual cramps, PMS, migraine headaches or some other body event which cannot be disputed for its real presence, but can be disputed for its real cause. The patient is wheezing and does have diarrhea. But these are, as one analyst put it, "the tears and sweat of the lungs and bowels." They are shouting at us in a language which neither they nor we are able to fathom. Unless nursing or psychoanalysis is your hobby or life vocation, you are better off to effect your departure from these partners real early, especially if you have even a modest sexual appetite. However else these maneuvers may complicate your interpersonal life, they provide enormous resistance to a good sex life—"You animal, you! Can't you see I'm sick?"

A careful analysis of psychosomatic illness reveals it to often be just another form of bitching and so, unhitching from it is a safety net for both of you. Yes, I said both of you, because the person doing the bitching is also better left alone and free from the inevitable stresses of relationships, for which they are ill prepared and which aggravate their already preexisting impairments. In most instances, you do your partner a favor by leaving.

There is a darker side to this story, for when psychosomatic bitching doesn't work, the blackmail of other, more radical, self-destructive behaviors is just around the corner. Yes, I'm talking about suicidal threats and gestures, the overdose of pain killers and alcohol as "the only thing that lets me sleep" or "reduces the pain." Threats of such behavior are extremely intimidating and have kept many couples together by such blackmail and extortion.

Some readers are probably thinking that I have forsaken my psychiatric brethren with these heathen outbursts. Do I not trust a one of them to treat or save my normal readers from psychoneurotic or psychosomatic partners?

The answer is both yes and no. Yes, I do believe that psychotherapy, pharmacotherapy and behavior modification techniques are useful in helping people "grow up," by forsaking such unconscious, self-destructive mechanisms of psychological defense as well as these psychophysiological reactions. And, when they do, perhaps it will be appropriate to try again to have a relationship with them. In the meantime, let them impose this behavior onto some other guy or gal, because as long as you stay, it's too easy to transfer the blame and not fix what's really broken. Your departure says, "Grow up; I don't need this. I don't deserve this."

From my point of view, it's as fraudulent to forget to tell your intended that you had your tubes tied, have herpes, or were married before and have two kids, as it is to not confide that you are phobic of airplanes or hate homosexuals or have psychosomatic colitis, sick headaches, sexual frigidity or impotence. Sexual frigidity you ask? I know that sounds silly in this day and age, but "faking" sexual interest or pleasure in courtship is just another one of the psychophysiological, bitching games that bitching partners play!

In chapters to follow I will talk more about these mechanisms but, more importantly, I will teach you strategies for achieving either of the two major goals of this text:

1. Avoiding bitching relationships in the first place;
2. Exiting from those that already exist.

4

Love's Enemies:
False Premise and "To Me" Thinking

*"But the mortalist enemy unto knowledge and that which
hath done the greatest execution upon truth hath been a
peremptory adhesion into authority and more especially the
establishing of our belief upon the dictates of antiquity."*

—*Thomas Brown*
Enquiries into Vulgar and Common Errors

Now that you have some perspective on methods of psychological defense, we can now discuss two other processes which are too pervasive to meet the formal definition of a mental mechanism, but which cast the same dangerous shadow over personal relationships—false premises and the "to me" phenomenon.

The attention of early psychoanalysts was so taken with the long march down the royal road to the unconscious by the goose-step rituals of dream analysis and free associations that such simple explanations as false facts and premises often escaped their attention. However, cultural bias, language, confusion and misinformation which are the derivatives of false premise produce as severe an encumbrance to self awareness and a proper perception of the world around us as do unconscious mental mechanisms.

Inability to identify errors of perception, belief or misinformation about those others with whom we consort is as hazardous to our ability to have successful relationships with them as phobia, projection and repression. Therefore, they also play a major role in most bitching relationships.

The feelings of emancipation and euphoria on the face of a child lost in a large store as the manager reunites the child with the frantic mother will serve as a metaphor for the role that clarification plays in psychotherapy. In my practice, relief from the burden of a wrong idea or a false premise is as much a factor of therapy as guiding a patient from the lost department of id to the place of ego, and the resultant emotion which accompanies the integration of the new truth is very much like being found when you are lost.

Simply showing someone where they are wrong in their perception of why something is the way it is, or relieving them of the burden of misunderstanding that what they thought to be so is not, can bring the same relief of tension and renewed optimism as in the example of the lost child.

No student of the human condition understood this better or said it more precisely than the Harvard philosopher and pragmatist Charles Saunders Pierce. "It's terrible to see how a single unclear idea lurking in a young man's head like an obstruction of inert matter in an artery hindering the nutrition of the brain, condemns its victim to pine away in the fullness of his individual vigor. Many a man has cherished for years some vague shadow of an idea too meaningless to be positively false. He has nevertheless passionately loved it, leaving all other occupations for its sake, flesh of his flesh, bone of his bone."

Yes, flesh of his flesh, bone of his bone, that's how tenaciously many individuals hold to their childhood remnant hypotheses and formulas as to why what is is. This is especially true in their interpersonal lives. Thus, a critical element of my practice is teaching them to "let go." But as one patient so poetically put it as she likened herself to a trapeze performer, "You can't let go without a net of reassurance stretched taut below you or the strong, outstretched arms of your trusted partner on the opposite trapeze swing, or else you will come crashing down to the cement below." Such a partner describes well the new role of the modern psychotherapist and family counselor.

A few examples from my practice can make this point more emphatic.

In a recent group psychotherapy session, Mary asked those present not to smoke. Laura replied, "How can someone who has lived with a man to whom she is not married for two and a half years dare ask somebody else not to smoke?"

What we have here is a conflict of premises. Mary did not want chemical pollutants in her lungs or on her clothing. Laura questioned her moral entitlement to such an indulgence. Who could have known yesterday that Laura owned this peculiar moral equation, i.e., ladies who sleep with men to whom they are not married are not entitled to clean air.

I assure you that Laura is not a unique owner of unusual quid pro quo formulas. It's amazing how many unusual and false premises or beliefs are owned by even our best friends. However, without a stress to reveal them, they lie dormant. It is only under stress that we are confronted with the shallow river of reason or knowledge upon which most people attempt to move the cargo of their arguments or, for that matter, manage their daily lives in general.

These ideas were conveyed to us by those same parental and preparental ancestors who taught us right from wrong, could from can't, true from false, pretty from homely, bad from good, and OK from not OK. Remember when we were kids, how angry we became if anyone said anything bad about our mothers? Like they were wrong or may be dumb or, God forbid, sexual. Why, we would knock them right off their bike even if they were the biggest bully in the school yard. "No one talks about my mom that way," we would cry out as we charged with caution to the wind. When the family honor was at stake, we would risk a bloody nose to defend it.

Have you noticed how far into the adult years and how tenaciously most people still hang on to their favorite ideas in debate or dialogue with others, as if by disagreeing with them we had said something unkind about their mothers? Why do you think this is so? Why shouldn't folks be able to tell us that our mother may have made a mistake? We ask our missionaries to do this all the time when they go into cultures other than their own.

In my practice, I have learned that people hold no more tenaciously to their neurotic mechanisms of psychological defense than they do their private beliefs and premises. They are no different in this respect than those headhunting aborigines who would not relinquish their folk ways, myths or heroes when proselytized by Christian missionaries.

Whether it be to hang on to a primitive belief which cannot bear the weight of the science and experience of later generations or hold to a false current premise or neurotic mechanism of psychological defense, this tenacity is a major underlying factor for almost all bitching relationships. This is so because in many people's lives, winning arguments has become more important than knowing what is true. This is so because in the heat of dialogue, the worry that if I am not right I do not exist prevails over the goal of intimacy. It is then that many people behave as if their life depended upon an issue that to others appears quite petty.

Beware of those folks. Their very being is brittle, and they are made of the Tinkertoys of simple sentences and primitive logic. They do not know that that cannot be a fact of theirs which is not a fact at all. They have not learned that no two objects can occupy "the same place at the same time." They don't believe it. Since feeling is first, they pay no attention to the syntax of things. They are in the sandbox. They believe that when an object cannot be seen by them, it does not exist. The shadow of a bathrobe upon the nursery wall really is a bear, and no fluorescent or standard light will assuage their fear. No high school babysitter will do until mother comes home. Only mother can change the formula and replace the myths of childhood with her unique warmth and tenderness.

Why is this so? The answer is simply because it once was unequivocally true that death was the only alternative to mother's absence. She was the whole world of feelings, ideas, will and wishes, and we were in her hands.

Some of us have never figured out that it doesn't have to still be that. Perhaps this point is better made by noting that some folks did not have parents who realized that mammalian dependence which was so suited to the development of our frontal lobes was only temporary, and that someday we would leave home with brains, ideas and feelings of our very own.

"Proprius manibus," Galen shouted from the gallery as he rushed to the autopsy table—"with my very own hands." Let me touch this anatomical fact with my very own hands. I cannot sit in the gallery and learn medicine by hearing and seeing how others do it. I must do it myself.

I must learn from the facts which my own hands have grasped.

Am I saying, "Rid your lives of all learned values?" Am I saying, "The religions of the patriarchs, the Sermon on the Mount, the Book of the Dead are outdated for truth and wisdom?" Of course not. What I am saying is that you have a right to read them anew in light of your adult years. Some truths may beam even more brightly. But, and here's the rub, some may pale and fade. We must each write our own Talmud for our own bible. To achieve the glory of our adulthood, we must rid our lives of the premises which enabled us to be good children.

The second category of this chapter of those severe impediments to interpersonal joy, and a basic element of many bitching relationships, is the "to me" phenomenon. Eavesdrop on this conversation, and then we shall analyze its contents:

Son: Hello, Mom. I'm so happy. Everything that I believed you ever told me that was good and pleasing and life-affirming has occurred. I'm in medical school studying to be a specialist, and I have found a girl who makes me very happy. She seems to respect my needs for privacy when I study, is very undemanding, an excellent cook, gorgeous and sensitive and, in her own right, quite intelligent and self-sufficient. Oh yes, she's law review at her law school.

Jewish Mom: (long pause) ... Is she Jewish?

Son: No, Mother.

Mom: (longer, perhaps eternal pause) ... How could you do that to Me?

What most folks, and this mother, don't know is that most people do things to and for themselves, not others. It is a hazardous and erroneous presumption to assume the behavior of another is a "to you" event. It is proper to say, "When you do that I feel bad." To believe that because of how you feel the other person should not do that, or that the other person did that so you would feel bad, is presumptuous at best. Often, that can be the key to awareness of your persistent juvenile ideas of entitlement rather than citizenship in the adult state. The son has a new relationship to a lady friend—a new diad of their interest in one another is being formed. But alas, it turns out to be a triangle. His brains, and those of many others, are infected with "third-party" guilt-ghosts which haunt the mind, whispering judgments about behavior, setting guidelines, and labeling actions as correct and nice or selfish and cruel to others who are watching and judging them. Who wrote these contracts which we only now know we signed when we were too young to comprehend their articles, let alone read the small print of their references.

The answer is mostly the moms and pops, or their equivalents, of the formative years. In asking, "How could you do this to me?" this mom is saying that her son has missed the small print in their contract. "Only as long as it pleases me, you dummy!" is what she is saying. "I want you to be happy only in my world and at my table." By picking a shiksa he is betraying her sacrifices and blaspheming her motherly efforts. He is defying the relationship duties which he only now knows have always been present but sequestered under the comforter of what's good for us first may then be good for you.

The mom can then assert and prove by sacred logic that the failure of the father's business, the crash of the stock market, the sinking of San Francisco into the San Andreas Fault, will all follow as a direct result of the son's rebellion. And the son, by ritual of circumcision, bar mitzvah and the food of festive holidays is now engulfed by a tidal wave of guilt and self-incrimination.

Having programmed this reflex in her son, i.e., he must obey her in order to maintain her love and avoid her loss, she can now harvest her crop of duty. While this has not been yet identified as a legal cause of death, "This will kill your mother" is a fever which few remedies have been known to break.

The still-dependent child in the son responds to the guilt-inducing disapproval of Mom. He is now engaged in a dramatic internal battle between acceptance of the value and world system of Mom and his belief in his own adult decision-making abilities.

The determining factor in one's guilt response quotient is the degree to which the illogical, unthinking guilt reaction (to parental labeling of a "no-no") becomes replaced by an ability to decide, for oneself, whether or not there has been a real violation of a rational adult ethic chosen by the now-adult/then-child. "This thing I want is good and right and does not contradict my value system. Therefore, fearing it as a Mama's no-no is ridiculous!"

Many bitching transactions are derived from these early triangles, i.e., you, the other, plus a special third ghost whose neurotic relationship to your bitching partner is easily reincarnated by stress.

So, what's the bottom line? Be careful of the haunted houses in which such players live. You don't need to become a psychiatrist; merely become a better student of the interpersonal territory: a geographer of that space that separates you from others. When you train your observations to see these false premises and the other defenses that other persons in your life use, you will be able to discern when they speak from the freedom of the here and now or when they are in a triangle with you. You will come to know when feelings are original and creative or yesterday's warmed over.

You will come to know when a person's behavior is now or when he or she is acting as a child whose life literally does depend on parental approval. You will come to discern when it's not really you, the here-and-now partner, upon whom their interpersonal prosperity depends, it's them! This connection to yesterday's people is comprehended by some psychologists as transference. For them, transference underlies all prejudices in the free flow of interpersonal communication.

Transference is feelings and judgments projected upon here-and-now people from our recent and remote past, and it may be positive or negative. However, whether you are positively or negatively misperceived, whether it is labeled as a ghost from a primary triangle or transference, eventually reality will catch up with you.

You are not as heroic or as beautiful as they wish you were or as evil or as dangerous. You are just another folk, and it is only for your folksiness that you have any business being loved and appreciated or hated and despised. It is only when cleansed of transference, false premise and mental mechanisms of defense that you can be you. And they can be they. An incident which demonstrates these points occurred while I was psychiatric consultant to a design school in Rhode Island.

Well into her wedding plans, a tearful coed came to my office. "I can't go through with it," she wept. "I just can't." As the story evolved, the incident which provoked her tears clarified. She had just returned from the home of her future in-laws to go over the selection and outfitting of the bridesmaids. However, when her soon-to-be husband learned that she had asked a black high school classmate to be among them, he gave her a surprisingly hostile rebuke. "But Charlene and I were on the same volleyball team since grade school and it was Charlene who ran the blood donor program at our high school when my brother Joey was so sick," she retorted. "But she's Black," he explained, "and I don't think my two sisters can handle that."

"Doctor," she continued, "how could I ever be married to a man who vetoed a Black bridesmaid at his wedding?"

This is not so much an incident of false premise as it is an incident of sequestered or hidden premise, but the issue is the same. People can have important ideas and beliefs about almost anything which can thwart your personal intimacy with them, and while it is folly to believe that any formal preinventory could ever be prescribed to have precluded this or similar incidents, this point is certain. What we don't know about the people to whom we are connected can hurt us.

Another demonstration of this experience also took place at that design school. A young, recently married lad came to me to help him understand how or why his wife's ardor had so dramatically changed almost within minutes after their wedding. He was a scholarship student from a midwestern high school, gifted but naive, sensitive but simple. She, on the other hand, was a JAP—a Jewish American Princess, the darling of her father who was mayor of an upper class suburb, President of his Temple and a wealthy merchant.

In attempting to answer his question, "How could she do that to me?" I had to reply, "It had nothing to do with you, but everything to do with him." She did it for her father. For years she had conceded her identity to his will in their patriarchal family. She dressed to please him. She chose her college for him. She had her bas mitzvah for him. She was daddy's girl, but vowed to not be daddy's woman. So the cut had to be swift and final. She would marry a Christian! But at no time did she seriously consider being a wife to her husband—only a bride on her wedding day.

Could he have known this earlier? Probably not. What should he do now? Accept and run. "You have lived in an absurd world in which what you saw was not what was," I told him.

The pain of her husband was reactive to the displaced hostility she had harbored against her father. Her new husband was the displaced object of her adolescent rebellion against her father, and for the brief moments of her courtship, the ticket for her emancipation from a sinister triangle of which he had no knowledge nor for which he should have borne any pain.

This was a triangle in which the daughter had become surrogate wife to the needs of her father whose own wife, now overweight and very busy, had long since departed their bedroom for her committee work.

For a while it wasn't so bad. However, she soon learned that the price was too high for the constraints on her personal freedom. Party dresses, exclusive summer camps, and a shiny red sports car no longer could silence the questions, "Who am I? Where am I going?"

To the questions of these two design students, "How could they do that to me?" we now reply, "It was not to you but for them." The points of these stories, I hope, is clear. Nobody wins in human interpersonal intercourse when the "to me" game is played. So this issue is always relevant in serious relationships, i.e., who else lies under the covers or sits across the room besides me and my partner and what business is this of theirs?

There is, however, an upside of this equation—it's not all bad, it's only when those others are neurotically involved with our partners that we need fear them. They can be our friends. They can also be saying "atta girl, atta girl" or "atta boy, atta boy. That's how to treat your lover," not just "what the hell are you doing with this joker? You should be home getting me a beer!"

Humor plays a role in false premise and "to me" relationships, for false premise and "to me" conversions of the innocent behavior of others often thrive on the bleak and boring plains of folks who have no sense of humor. Actually, humor is not a sense at all—it is a complex mental conversion of otherwise untouchable aggressive human energy. It lies fallow and dormant in the lives and hearts of those players who don't dare to call their relations a game—whose recreation and success phobia and psychosomatization reactions transform their flexible human faces into brittle and stiff stares. Their smiles are mostly from embarrassment, and their strict interpretation of the real world denies them the gigantic potential of laughing at cosmic absurdity and human frailty. An anecdote from the life of James Joyce may make this point a bit clearer.

While attending a Dublin cocktail party in honor of the great author, a young graduate student in English accosted him with these remarks. "Oh, Mr. Joyce," he exclaimed. "I am so thrilled to meet you. I've read everything you've ever written." "Thank you," Joyce replied, "and how did you like *Ulysses*?" "Oh sir, I'm reading it now for the third time and I'm just beginning to understand its dramatic themes and complex cross-references." To which Joyce is alleged to have asked, "Didn't you think it was funny?" Obviously not.

Although marital and relationship conflict and disagreements are obviously not funny when they occur, there is respite in our eventual ability to laugh at ourselves in such situations and to experience laughter as a catharsis for the other complicated feelings that otherwise attend disappointment, loss and confusion.

One of the most original authors on the subject of laughter was the psychoanalyst Martin Grotjohn. While not the first to notice, he provided a detailed analysis of laughter in everyday living and concluded, "Laughter provides for the release of aggression in a form which is socially acceptable." But to be effective, the humor must carry the aggression so well disguised and attractively expressed so as not to attack the adversary openly or directly. The joke without laughter, he taught, is no joke at all. If the disguise is too thin, hostility at worse and embarrassment at best will result. Such replies as, "That's not funny, Joe," or "What's so funny about that, Jane?" can usually be heard when this anger has been poorly masked and when the object of the humor has experienced the underlying hostility. When someone has tried to be funny and failed, somebody else is usually hurt. OK, you may ask, what does this have to do with bitching? The answer is "everything!"

Early in the analysis of a bitching relationship, it is clear that those couples have lost or never had the capacity to find any humor route to decompress the inevitable tension of their relationship. By the time they come for therapy, humor has completely departed them as a technique for flushing out the inevitable anger and disappointment which attends all serious human encounters.

Freud also wrote about this circumstance in his essay "The Purpose of Jokes," where he saw the humorist as exquisitely sensitive to the world's misery and his own absurd plight. "But, he triumphs over it," Freud said, "with comic irreverence." Not only is humor an escape for aggression against others but an escape from aggression against ourselves.

A patient came to her fifth therapy session obviously depressed and more apprehensive about "us" than on her four prior visits. It wasn't long before she accused me of having "laughed at her" in our previous session. She recalled telling me of an embarrassing incident of her childhood—a school toilet she had just used failed to flush, and she had been transfixed by the fantasy that her whole class would see her feces. When she returned to the classroom, she convulsed into tears believing that her secret was known to all and that they were disgusted with her. Surely there was nothing funny about it then! However, after some discussion of its affective persistence through time and circumstance, I suggested, "Well, Marylou, after 28 years maybe in your therapy we can finally flush that toilet and your shame and embarrassment down the commode at last—with a smile." She didn't think this was helpful at all, certainly nothing to smile about, and she was right. On that visit it wasn't. But if she is ever to get "well," it will someday have to be more funny and less tragic.

Not "ha ha" funny, but funny like the laughter that follows the news that the tumor is benign.

The tragedy of this lady is that she has not learned to extricate herself from childhood aggressive impulses. By insisting that there is still nothing funny about her past she is saying much more. She is saying, "There is no way out of eternal bondage and anger for the insults of my childhood, there is no exit from the triangles of my past."

I wanted desperately to inject some humor into her situation. Surely we can all empathize with the original insult to her delicate psyche, but it was time to invite humor into her life. I can envisage that timid, desperately frightened child in the classroom thinking that all the Gods on Olympus were convulsively laughing at her poo-poo. I tried to insinuate a smile to incise that boil of memory but failed. She thought I and they were still laughing at her. Her memory told her that they were laughing at her then. Her neurosis was telling her that they still are. Her repression of the shame of that day had encapsulated into today's bitterness. Humor could not breathe into those constricted lungs. Perhaps in our next session she and I will do a psychodrama of the incident and, through her tears of recollection, we'll find something to smile about!

Neither time alone nor hindsighted laughter had provided an escape valve for those hurts. Marylou saw her childhood as having a terrible eternal reality which could not be reversed. She had not yet learned that though there was nothing funny about the original events, the psychological process of humor lets us emotionally rewrite our history. Those things were not happening to her now. She lived in a time warp, still nude to those arrows which can pierce the flesh of children but should be dull to the character armor of adults.

It is not only that humor allows us to decompress the hurt of the immediate slap on our ego's face, but it permits us to get out from behind grudge and vengeance, those volcanoes of wasted energy which keep us in yesterday.

When I first taught the residents in psychiatry at Boston University in the late 1950s, I said that the two essential traits of a good psychiatrist are (1) a good sense of humor and (2) love for a good story. I have come to appreciate over the ensuing years this critical addendum—ability to make an old story better by re-ending it with a smile!

We can't change our history, but we can reinterpret it. We can dilute its stark and ancient crimson to mauve. You see, everyday humor and laughter in our lives reveals our ability to creatively and constructively reexamine and then rewrite our ancient history. Its absence keeps us in the mire of eternal seriousness. Nobody's childhood was funny to the children that they were, but yesterday's fears over spilled or lost milk must somewhere convert to play or laughter if we are ever to really enjoy a new day or new relationship.

The difference between complaining and bitching is thus made quite simple. Complaints are today. Bitching is the geometric transfer of energy to anything or anybody which still lives in our past and who, by analog or whim, can be resurrected and pinned as today's jackass.

And now to close this chapter, a superb example of the success of humor. As sprightly a 91-year-old lady as you are ever likely to meet came into my office from HRS the same day as Marylou. Her story was that she was quick-deeded out of her house by a greedy granddaughter and the granddaughter's "druggy" husband, as well as a $10,000 Certificate of Deposit for which she had scrimped from waitress jobs. Strokes and pneumonia had rendered her husband all but bedridden for the last 20 years of their 45-year marriage before his death 10 years ago.

"Do you read the paper, Elizabeth?" I asked, the format question to my standard mental competency exam to see if she was oriented in time, place and person. "Just the hard luck stories," she answered. "I like to see who is suffering like me, who's cheating on who, what crimes they commit, how they get caught and what punishments they get." Her smile, laughter and gestures were infectious and inspirational. But I could not tarry with the pleasure of her company, I had to proceed to my inquiry of her ability to think abstractly.

"Elizabeth," I asked, "what do folks mean when they say every cloud has a silver lining?" "Well," she said, "mine just turned to *brass*." I replied, "How do you keep your sense of humor, Elizabeth?" To which she responded, "It's that or die, Doctor," and damn it, if that's not the truth.

5

Bonding and the Unbonded
Who Can't Love

Elaborating on the anthropological work of Konrad Lorenz, psychologist Selma Fraiberg taught that the parent–child relationship in humans is the instrument by which our natural aggressive urges are socialized. She also explained the consequences of a failure to secure such a bond. She showed how our mechanisms of managing aggression turn on how well or poorly we were bonded to caring, responsible adults during our formative years. She taught how the emotionally traumatic loss of a caring parent by the child not only produces juvenile depression but limits the child's future ability to control aggressive responses to the inevitable stress of future losses.

The reason which Fraiberg propounded is simply: to preserve the caring person's relationship to us, we had to learn at critical stages in our growth and development to modify and temper our natural aggressive impulses toward them. The equation is quite simple. They are too precious for us to dare to lose by our aggressive behavior.

However, if the fates took such a caring person from us or if those persons are not sufficiently caring for us to be bonded to them during this critical period of early growth, then our rationale to control that aggression is diminished and our aggression is permitted to endure untamed. Fraiberg observed that if one manages to physically survive despite the absence of such a nurturing bond, then "a sad breed of humorless, aggressive, emotional robots can emerge, chronically dissatisfied with all future relationships and dangerous to themselves and others."

This chapter calls attention to the possible presence of such persons in our lives and the futility of endeavoring to solve such profoundly serious generic problems with here and now contracts of give and take. Those players in the interpersonal arena require extensive character analysis to alter their lifestyles. They only, as one author put it, wear the masks of sanity.

Prior to Fraiberg's work, most people believed that practically all children were provided such a humanizing bond in the course of their formative years. However, Fraiberg and other researchers have reported a much higher incidence of aberrant, aggressive behaviors in the so-called nonattachment mental illnesses of children. They have shown that without such initial parental bonding, major incapacities to form later bonds ensue. Observers of those people note that endeavors to relate to them "gives one an eerie feeling of non-contact." It is as if a desert, a Sahara of interpersonal space, surrounds them. Their life histories reveal that without such formative bonds, few if any other persons of significance ever enter their world. They live in spaces censored of joy, grief, remorse, and guilt. Their partners are found and replaced as objects with characteristic sameness, i.e., their partners are not known for who they really are but only as objects of service or instruments of gain and relief. Another terrifying characteristic of such individuals is their total absence of self-observation, self-criticism, and a pathetic failure to be able to receive the baton of humor with a smile (which will be addressed later).

From this stark introduction you may think that such individuals are destined to become vagrants occupying our slums, second-class rooming houses, mental institutions and state prisons or engaged in worldly enterprises where the absence of human attachment can afford vocation and specialization. But you are only partly right. Many degrees of this interpersonal deadness occur within many other individuals and become major factors in bitching relationships. No amount of caring or giving today will ever be adequate to fill the hollowness of their experiences of having been someone whom not even their mothers could love, care for or bond to. Furthermore, by endeavoring to connect to them, you in your frustration may also become the bitching partner until you learn that there is no one home beyond those scary eyes.

It is particularly sad to realize that when we talk about non-bonding or present-but-not-accounted-for parents, we are not talking about the witch mothers of fairy tales. We are talking about a sad, frightened group of parents, as varied as the teenaged, undernourished mothers of Harlem or Appalachia who are too hungry themselves to care or share the limited bounty of their pale bodies or unfurnished flats with their premature and soon-to-be unbonded offspring and the rich and famous parents who assign the critical tasks of mothering to starched or hired housemaids whose non-touching techniques of immaculate correction are as dilute of nourishment as tap water.

This failure to bond precurses and predetermines the next failure in the lives of these children, i.e., not learning to signal. It is in the bond that signals are first conveyed and comprehended.

The child's cry signals I am wet, I am cold, but if you change me I will feel better and I will not be disappointed or angry. If you reply to my signals of pain and need in a reliable predictable way, I will learn to adjust and temper my anger with you, since if I don't you may leave me and not feed me, not touch me—and I will die! If, however, my signals are only marginally met and unpredictably satisfied, if I do survive, I shall have despaired of trusting and lost my motive to give signals.

If you have been fated to know or to be connected to such a one as I have just described, don't expect more from them. Stop bitching as if they could and won't reach out and touch someone. They can't, and shouldn't be expected to. OK, if you want to be another Mother Theresa, that's fine—but know on day one that you are in a give-and-give-again relationship with them, and they are in a take-and-take-again one with you! The point is that the bond is the civilizing process for all human relationships. It neutralizes aggression, it begins communication. Interpersonal values derive their quality and meaning from these crucial early development experiences! Thus, in assessing your adult relationships, consider the story of the bonding experiences of your co-player. If you want to have a relationship where natural inborn aggression is reliably and appropriately socialized and managed, take a look at the bonding history of your co-player. If you want to have your signals read and appreciated, look at the bonding relationship history of your partner.

Rephrased, the point is ultimately simple: at some point in our species development we lost the genetic endowment for the skills and structure of spontaneous self-sufficiency at birth. Thus it was that we were beholden for our survival needs to giant others who nursed us to self-sufficiency. Those agents of nurture were also mentors of culture. Is it any wonder, then, that separation from them and death were etched into the same granite sentence: If they leave I will die! Yes, child rearing is a physical and cultural life or death transaction and the delivery system is interpersonal. There's food, warmth, medicine and language out there, but it must be delivered by another. The deliverers will either be on time or late. As they tarry, the primordial angers and fears will surface. As they arrive on time, faith and trust will form. Memory will punch in the joys and pains of these incidents of communion where tension was followed by relief, hunger by satiety, cold by warmth, wet by dry, alone with touching, and cries and sighs with words and deeds of comfort.

Thus we see that a careful understanding of our partner's earliest human relationships is crucial, for no inventory is more likely to provide useful information concerning your bitching involvements than this. What kind of bonds did they secure? What kind of bonds did they observe? OK, you reply, I know that what you say makes a lot of sense, but things are so different with Jannie. Yes, she was born on a mountaintop in Tennessee or a housing project in the Bronx; yes, she was left alone for days at a time to fend for herself; yes, uncles and neighbors took sexual advantage of her; yes, she was an underachiever in grade school, missing most of her classes with flu and earaches. Yes, by age 17 she had found in drugs or alcohol temporary respite from it all. But she has triumphed. She better than anyone knows how bad it can be, and more than anyone, knows not to replicate herself into those sad mother or wife molds. Oh, how I wish you were right, dear reader, but you are wrong. You are not wrong for every one unique exceptional poor Jannie, but for the statistical poor Jannies of the world. Without arduously long experiences of rehabilitation and character reconstruction they will become their mother's clone. (This applies to the poor Johnnies of the world becoming their poor father's clone as well.) You can't give what you didn't get.

Psychiatric and pastoral relationships are for "saving" or rehabilitation. Our everyday relationships are for something else—aren't they? What I'm emphasizing here is that unhitching from bitching begins with an acknowledgment of the power of the formative past of those with whom we are engaged. Without such knowledge, we cannot determine their capacity to be OK in their relationships with us.

No, you don't need to understand how they resolved their Oedipus or Electra complexes, just as beauticians don't need to learn cosmetic surgery to know how to comb hair or paint nails. But the more you know about how someone was raised, supported, challenged, threatened, taken through the critical states of anonymity into personhood—how they secured survival techniques for living as an adult, how and to whom they were bonded, who taught them how to express their existence, who were their models, who their devils—the more likely are you to avoid a bitching connection.

Let's garner more information on the signaling and bonding facts of life. No, not where do babies come from, but more importantly, where do adults come from? Those are the critical facts of life which most children crave. Those are the facts which will be most helpful to the formation of their adult personalities. Those are the facts of the true feelings and ideas which existed in the lives of those who raised them. It is not the biology of fertilization or the techniques of sexual consummation that children crave. It is what adults are all about.

Children don't need to hear about the private happenings in adult bedrooms anywhere near as early as they are entitled to know what is otherwise going on in the kitchens and dens of their households, i.e., the frustrations, disappointments, angers, hopes and aspirations of all the family players.

The full range of the human transactions witnessed by the child must be tested so that the child's impression can be validated or repudiated with the truth of what was actually happening in the interpersonal lives of those who raised him! Child rearing should above all else be honest. Its worst violation is the double message. Of course, the input of truth must be carefully timed and customed to the perceptive talents of the growing child and he must be helped to accommodate the news. Johnnie and Jannie must not only be taught how to be well-behaved children, but they must be permitted some news about how well-behaved adults comport themselves.

A critical item in this regard is providing children with a reliable vocabulary of feelings. In my practice I often see people with amorphously painful feelings which are immediately assuaged by assigning them a name. I have learned how valuable it is to have a language of one's emotional life, and, once named, how important it is to conjugate the verbs and decline the nouns of all the feelings which we endure. For this task nothing can replace the bond to a reliable adult.

The language of feelings provides a crucial restraint on our primitive emotions. If we do not master the process of translation of emotions to words, but rely on emotional reflexes during our formative hours, then we are forever vulnerable to our primitive and primate nature. Only in parent–child bonds can this occur.

As one reels back from the blunt pain of a physical assault, an observer may comment, "I think he's trying to tell you he doesn't like you!" Perhaps if he could say it, he wouldn't have to do it. This observation sounds so simple but it is so true. Yes, if we could first send or trust the scouts of language, words of feeling-into the dangerous interpersonal frontier, I am convinced that we would all be spared many of the harsh and painful bitching relationships that we have known.

In my practice, again and again I have witnessed individuals searching desperately for a word or a term to capture an otherwise overwhelming and exhausting intrapersonal feeling. When I succeed in discovering the words of clarification, I have been rewarded to see a new peace and calm settle upon my patients simply because they have found a way of collecting their feelings into the urns of language. However, what works in one psychotherapy session is not a formula for a lifetime of fixing such a person in a bad marriage.

For those deprived in their formative years of such translators by absence or abuse, by direct hostility or covert deprivations of silence and neglect, these processes of bonding and signaling often are irrevocably impaired. Reflex replaces cognition and insight. Thus deprived, they have no capacity for true intimacy. They will also bring out the bitch in you. Having previously failed to connect, they will know no better way to signal for your concern or interest than with the whining of their still-unsatisfied infantile selves or the irrational hostility of their juvenile delinquency.

Please, please let go of them and let them let go of you. They have graduate student needs—you are a primary school apprentice. Go to someone from your own town. No, don't marry your sister. Just someone who is bonded like you were to someone like your mom and pop!

6

Before We Can Love Them, We Have to Know Who They Are

It no more follows from the truth of such statements as, "I am five feet tall" that a person is his body, than it follows from the truth of such statements as, "I am out of gas" that a person is his automobile! —S. Shoemaker

It is one thing to be the same substance; another to be the same man; and a third to be the same person. —John Locke

I am not that set of limbs called the human body. —Descartes

Folks will be folks. —E. Semrad

Now that the concept of bonding and its relationship to identity has been presented, we are ready for an extended inquiry into what other factors determine who are the folks to whom we are attracted or attached.

This chapter says that those special persons with whom we quest for friendship, compatibility, and yes, love, can only be a subset of what persons actually are to begin with. It then asserts that most folks haven't given that much thought. In fact, most folks dismiss such simple inquiry as silly, while wallowing in what we shall soon identify as dangerous delusions. Our suggestion is that in order to do this, one must get into a philosophical mode of thinking and listening. This means nothing more than learning that the more beautiful answers follow the more beautiful and simple questions. Let's ask some simple questions about ourselves and our neighbors, and let's see what we can find out about normal and bitching relationships.

Misunderstanding the definition of person can be as devastating in keeping us in bitching transactions as almost any other intellectual or neurotic fault or habit.

I shall begin by simply saying, "There is no such thing as a person." There are only our opinions and beliefs about what a person is. In order to understand your relationship to someone, you must begin by understanding your ideas and beliefs about what that person is.

We shall begin, however, by saying that there are such things as bodies. Therefore, let's talk a little about bodies as introduction to our discussion of persons. Bodies are composed of cells and tissues which combine into organ systems which support the lives of persons who live in and by them and who are of them. Those cells, tissues and organ systems of the bodies of those persons deliver the realities of the outside world via processes called tasting, smelling, hearing, seeing and touching. This information is psychophysiologically encoded and factually and emotionally labeled and organized through processes called remembering, learning and reasoning. Then, by some magnificent leap, minds and persons with beliefs, ideas, feelings and attitudes emerge from the things that are bodies. Quite separate from any religious formula which explains this miracle, we know that these persons exist, only in their own special places at their own special times, and we can know some very important truths about both place and time. We can learn much about how they develop unique minds and personalities from inherited bodies and brains and, more importantly, we can learn much from discovering who cared enough to see that they got from those special places where they have been to this unique place in which they presently reside.

"What is this, a geography class?" you may ask. Well, in a way it is. This chapter identifies not only issues of what a person is but concepts of interpersonal space and time. It will show how knowledge of that space and time provides knowledge of how to achieve intimacy with those folks, but also when it's time to leave them.

Personal place is not just town and street. Place comprehends values and memories. It is a vast collection of premises, beliefs, and presuppositions. We all exist in a cultural place where such concepts as friendship and personal relationships, thought of love and justice, hypotheses about cause and effect in both nature and human behavior are crucial facts. These facts will carry us far beyond conventional oversimplification when they are reconsidered with the insights of this text. For example, Johnny may be more distant from his mother when he is at home than Joey is when he is away at school.

When Freud taught that the unconscious has no clock or compass, he was talking about this very issue. While one's body may be in one time space, the person to whom you wish to connect may be in quite another. He may be, for example, in a state of remorse or regret for a recent past loss or a remote past error. Likewise, he may be anxious about an immediate future event or prayerful about his remote future.

Perhaps these everyday examples will help clarify this point. For me, it's one o'clock in the afternoon of July 16, and I am reviewing a chapter of my book. What time is it for you? You may be in a delayed grief reaction to the death of your beloved mother who died this very day six years ago. Clearly we are in two different time zones and, if I want to understand my relationship to you, I must know what time it is for you. Another example of this from my practice concerns the devastated young coed who several weeks before her marriage learned that her fiancé objected to a black bridesmaid. "How could I be happy," she wept, "with someone who was in that place?" Prince Charles realized this when he identified his criteria for selecting a spouse to be the next Queen of England. He said that "she should be someone who is accustomed to living in a manor house." Right on, Prince! That's how to pick a queen. You need to know if she will fit into your place. More through the pain of exit than on entry do we realize the importance of the concepts of time and place in our relationships.

The unhitching from bitching task is a journey from a time-space of pain and suffering to one of respite where the self can be reevaluated. There is, however, no non-thinking route out of such interpersonal ties, though it does appear that most people would rather wallow in emotional despair than take the trouble to think their way out. Why? Because most people don't trust their brains when it comes to relationships. They will buy every consumer journal or government guideline when buying a new washer, but in the interpersonal realm they are dangerous gamblers. They love, in some tragic way, the game of chance in making the most important selections in their life. They act as if their intellect is a newcomer trying to take over primordial land granted sacred property. They are old-brain-dominant folks, believing that if thinking was so important to God, He wouldn't have let us breathe or pump blood without thinking about it. They act as if they also believe that God wants us to be where we are in bitching relationships bearing only what He knows we can. They argue that there must be something divine about the way it is or else there wouldn't be so many of us complaining about the rest of us.

It isn't customary to challenge new acquaintances to articulate their life journey or philosophy in the early hours of romantic or friendship encounters. Nonetheless, I submit that the longer we delay an honest discussion of the value-place of our new acquaintances, the longer we defer our interest about how they have sojourned to become the persons they appear to be. The less we are concerned about the beliefs and formulas which govern the special world in which they reside, the less likely are we to have genuinely successful relationships with them!

Conversely, the more likely are we to interbitch with them. Yes, we are not only entitled to ask questions about the moral places they have been, but we must know the moral decisions they have made. Their personhood, who they are, derives from these decisions.

I would love to tarry here and dialogue with those who believe otherwise—who insist that essence precedes existence; who argue that we are all original sinners, but lovable by a forgiving God. But as I say so often in my practice, "If your religious beliefs can sail you safely through the troubled waters of your interpersonal lives, then I will not contest that victory." However, for those of you who aspire to live in a world where reality can be tested, where truth can be measured, and where doing is worth more than saying; for those of you who choose to live in a world where being is begotten of choice and where friendship and love should turn on performance, you must pay attention to these ideas of persons, places and times.

I am reminded again of the experience of that medical student who, after a summer separation from his ladyfriend, learned that she had fallen in love with a basketball player at a summer resort. In her zeal to explain her behavior, she announced, "I know we had a very nice relationship, but I never saw you in stress." When he replied, "Well, how am I doing?" it was too late. She was already "in love" with someone else. He had missed her moral stress test, but her idea wasn't such a bad one. Too bad she hind-placed its use and didn't wait to find out if his grief mechanisms were adequate to cope with the necessary losses which invariable occur in all human relationships.

Another anecdotal incident in my practice where someone's not knowing their place contributed to their disunion may also prove helpful in making this point.

A patient recalled that on a weekend tryst with her new boyfriend, while she was in the ladies' lounge, he removed what he considered to be a gaudy attachment on her bathing cap.

"How dare you," she screamed when she returned, "decide what kind of a bathing cap was right for me? You had no business taking that flower off my bathing cap. You had no idea what it meant to me." Poor Joe! All he knew was that the flower was loose and didn't fit his idea of beauty. He had only his bias and misjudgment to rely on. He actually thought he was helping. Without remedy, guys like Joe are in for a lot more interpersonal trouble. They don't know where they are in their relationships with their ladyfriends or what time it is.

In the skirmishes and full battles between spouses, lovers, and friends, situations such as Joe's are found over and over. A misunderstanding of how far we may move into another's space without trespassing, or misunderstanding how important things are to the significant others in our lives, is serious business. Recognizing this is a vital skill which this chapter should help sharpen. These seemingly petty misunderstandings have a profound theme, namely that it is crucial to comprehend first and respect second the complexity of the experience of going into someone else's place. For the reader of this chapter, "Your place or mine?" will never again be a simple question. Although it is not necessary to immediately undertake a philosophical inquiry into their views on God, genetics, time, space, or ethics, you must surely recognize that you join another at your peril without some concern for these matters.

It not only takes a great deal of caring to be well placed with another, it takes a great deal of knowing. Assumptions, presumptions, and intuition are unreliable guideposts for this task. We must humble ourselves to realize that what you feel you've got is only what you feel you've got. However fascinating it may be to have feelings which leave you speechless, you must be able to think about them. Realize that though they may be your true feelings, they will only bear the weight that a feeling bears, and in reality, feelings bear little weight. They don't let you pass tests. They won't feed babies. They are the accessories to important decisions, packed after your thinking shoes for your life's climb.

If you were lost in a forest, you wouldn't dare act on the feeling that north was to the left without checking your compass, would you? No matter how powerful that feeling was! Or would you? So in your feeling relationships, think time, think place, think journey from before to now, think from now to where. Only then will you know who this person really is. Yes, that's a person you're trying to get along with. Do you know what that is? And in endeavoring to answer that question, do you realize that no data can ever be separated from the latent biases of the observer and the inherent limits of the deserving instruments? In understanding others, our perceptive lenses must be as free from the distortions of prejudgments as possible. How do we do this? We desist from considering others as human objects equivalent to ourselves by questing for their unique personhood as a derivative of our now-expanded concept that any person can only be a subset of what he or she believes persons to be.

Only in such subject–subject intercourse can we see others as coming from their own cultural and sociobiological pasts, not ours. Only in this way are we able to truly be with others in their places at their times. Only then can our connections to them be truly formulated.

In a recent magazine article, networking phone calls between adolescents was described. The authors noted how much more these youngsters were finding out about one another without the disadvantage or encumbrance of the chemistry of seeing each other.

The fascinating question which these experimental encounters attempted to answer was, "Can getting to know and like someone by talking to them sight unseen and touch unfelt, obliterate the bias of not liking their looks?" They say it worked with the elephant man. Shouldn't it work with us? Do we dare recommend it to our children? We know that not liking someone's looks can and surely has kept us from knowing their mind.

What the article revealed was the marvelous ability of these adolescents to communicate with one another without the apprehension or tension of pimply cheeks, small stature or, in some instances, blindness or lameness. The experimenters realized from their recorded conversations that the person could be emancipated from the body, and that profoundly important, and in some instances delightfully romantic, connections could be secured.

With this simple electronic gimmick, have we finally got the horse in front of the cart of human intercourse? With the tasks of encounter relieved of the transferences limits of physical attractiveness or homeliness, personality and intelligence could become romantically attractive. The person comes alive. Person, time and place are given a new focus. Impulse and intuition are replaced by ideas and beliefs. Sexual chemistry takes its rightful second place.

The next area to address is the continuity of persons in time with their necessary and essential properties. Now that you have a better understanding about a person's time and place, you are able to ask the next set of equally important but more sophisticated questions: "Which of a person's properties are necessary and essential, and how do those traits continue in time with them?" It was in a course with metaphysician Roderick Chisholm, years ago at Brown University, that I had my first occasion to consider these issues. Since then I have come to view them as not only "philosophical" topics, but as extremely practical "medical-psychiatric" issues. For example, I consider daily with my patients whether they and the special others in their lives are the same persons today as they were at fixed other points in the recent and remote past. Consider a 48-year-old patient. Surely he is not the same 19-year-old college sophomore who took

Genetics 103 and Physical Chemistry 112 so he could get into dental school. When he tells me about his college days, though, he says, "I did this" or "I did that." We both know it is not the same "I"—or is it? No, he is just continuous in time with that "I" and shares with no other "I" those memories. So what, you may ask. So this! If you want to know who I am now, you had better care about who I was, and how, and with what consistency of what self-parts, has the I of then become the I of now! No, I am not suggesting that a psychiatric question-naire be run to see whether I have had mood swings or schizophrenic deperson-alization, or psychotic excursions into paranoid delusions—though this data is not irrelevant, of course. I am simply saying that continuity of self is the mother of reliability and the father of trust. It is a powerfully important piece of infor-mation to have about someone, and you don't have to be ashamed to ask for it.

If you want to get out of, or never get into, a bitching relationship, you need to know a lot more about things like that.

Emerson (on a bad day, I guess) misconstrued the meaning and worth of personal consistency by calling it "the hobgoblin of average minds." Notwith-standing such a noble author's misconception, I contend that the measure of personal consistency and continuity in the lives of special others is an absolutely crucial dimension for assessing their worth and compatibility to us.

While some philosophers and other cynics can tell us "all things flow and nothing is," I submit that in our personal lives it behooves us to quest for pre-dictable and reliable traits, qualities, actions and reactions in those with whom we hope to have an endearing and enduring relationship. Not knowing what roman-tic turn or creative enterprise your partner may undertake, or not knowing by what metaphor he or she may depart reality, may be swell for a day. However, wholesome interpersonal relationships rely on the sure knowledge that however long you tarry in la-la land, truth, virtue, reliability, tenderness, and caring will persist in the business of the next day.

That is what bitches promise but can't produce.

The quality of a successful human relationship derives from the continu-ancy of these traits and virtues which both partners agree are the essential and respected properties of the other person. It is impossible to have a successful human relationship with someone who says, "Oh, I forgot to tell you I only behave the way I behave when I feel that way."

If you now wonder whether your partner is a role player with separate alli-ances, separate gamesmanship, and separate rules for different times and places, then this may be your moment of truth. Today you may begin your odyssey home. Separate from these role players—for bitching is their destiny.

Every serious participant in the interpersonal arena needs to know the difference between partners playing many roles and essential persons whose virtues endure, though there may be an occasional change of costume, through time and that they always know and are of their place. Once you or your partner establish personal and private understanding of those self-traits which you consider your essentialness, you entrust yourself into an identity from which becoming someone other is not the virtue of freedom, but the liability of inconsistency. On the other hand, to define all of your behavior as essential to your identity will make you so rigid in your presentation that you can only be related to as a solid object, incapable of the give-and-take potential which enriches all human interpersonal activity.

No measure of worth could be more useful in assessing the merits of an interpersonal relationship than how much you and your partners can and will change for a partner and with what tenacity essential virtues are held. What you and they come to learn about the elements and essential properties of your personhood is critical, both as protection against entering and facilitating your exit from a bitching relationship.

In questing to secure quality interpersonal contact or to exit unproductive and dangerous relationships, you must inquire, "Is my partner bound to his essential virtuous traits, yet is he secure and sufficiently self-identified by them to be free to negotiate the business of sharing by accommodating in all those other places in which the self given is the self enhanced?" A final illustration of this matter of necessary and essential properties and the personhood of our partners occurred in a recent marriage counseling session.

A couple, in their attempt to reconcile, were inventorying for me the merits and liabilities of their marriage. When the husband included sexual fidelity as among his virtues, the wife replied, "That's no big deal—you've got no choice!" What she meant was, since it's no problem, chore or effort for her husband to be sexually faithful ("that's the way he is"), his sexual fidelity was no great offering. She proceeded to argue that because it would be harder for him to be unfaithful than for him to remain faithful, his fidelity was no bargain. Her thesis was that since it is provided without sacrifice or strain, since he does it naturally, since it is essential to him, since he is continuous in time with this virtue, it has limited worth in their marital give and take. Her terribly false premise was that it is only giving if it hurts; you are giving only if you prefer to do otherwise but concede to the preference of another. To her, the issues of give and take turned on how much pain we endure in making changes to suit the needs of our partners, not how serious are our separate liabilities or how noble are our virtues.

She is wrong in focusing on the pain of change rather than the severity of the misbehavior as issue for negotiation. However, she does raise the extremely interesting point of giving and taking, which confounds most players in the interpersonal game, and deserves a little more discussion in this chapter.

"It's so easy for you, Joe," Jane says, "to be kind, generous and patient. You have so much security and power and self-esteem everybody likes you at work; your mom and your dad are so proud of you! On the other hand, how can you expect a poor orphan girl like me who never graduated high school, who hung her bathing suit on a nail at the public beach before 'big daddy' came along, how can you expect me to be a giver?" The answer is, of course, not easily or realistically. Joe should know, and if he doesn't he needs to be taught, that interpersonal giving does come from having. If you haven't got "it," you can't give, it, and having it comes from having gotten it from someone else when the self was being formed. And what exactly is this "it"? While it may be just the boy scout oath for others, to me the real stuff of "it" is trust, loyalty, friendship, courtesy, kindness, cheerfulness, thrift, bravery and reverence. If those are a couple's necessary and essential properties, if those are continuous in their time and define their place, then his chewing with his mouth open and her cracking her knuckles surely can be negotiated. But if they are not, why bother?

7

They Only Meant the Words They Said: A Response to Shere Hite's *Women and Love*

In the introduction to Shere Hite's book *Women and Love*, Professor Sullivan of the University of Minnesota states, "In short Hite has used a kind of intensive analysis method, but not of individuals—of attitudes and feelings. One might say that she is trying to put a whole society on the couch. Hers are works with many different purposes, and scholars and readers can use them in many different ways."

One way in which I shall use those purposes is to raise this question—does love have to be deserved? First, however, note that Hite's method was to send out 100,000 questionnaires consisting of 127 several-part questions, some with as many as seven parts per question. An example is "Question #118: What do you like about your closest woman friend? What do you do together? When do you see each other? Has she helped you through difficult times and vice versa? How do you feel when you are together? Do you have a good time? How much time do you spend together or talking on the telephone? What does she do that you like the least?"

Though her intent may have been to "provide a scientific sociopolitical and psychological assay of women," Hite's conclusions became no more than a codification of the inadequacies of men and a narrative of women's plight as disadvantaged players, and thus losers in the love game (a game which men also are ill-prepared to play).

From my perspective, the 4,500 responses to Hite's questionnaire provided a panoramic view of the misconceptions of both men and women of the reality of their relationships. Though the respondents' yearnings were clearly revealed, no serious inquiry into their entitlement to satisfaction was properly offered. It was submitted as a given, which for me posed this very important question: by what authority do these women or any of us deserve satisfaction from our partners? By whose decree do those women or their male partners deserve better than these disappointed and frustrated respondents? The sad answer to these questions is that most men and women in troubled relationships deserve each other, and most disappointments accrue not from the frustrations of just desserts but by the confrontation that infantile narcissistic entitlement fantasies must eventually give way to facts! While the format of Hite's book was women's answers to 127 questions, I hope to convey insights about love for both men and women. By commenting on the answers of Hite's respondents, I shall show that when most of these women, "whether married, single or divorced of all ages say they have not yet found the love they are looking for and that their greatest hope is yet to come," it is not love at all that they are talking about. As soon as they could learn that this is so, it would be so much easier for them to say goodbye.

My critique begins with noting 17 of Hite's statistical conclusions:

1. 98 percent of the women in this study say that they would like more verbal closeness with the men they love.

2. 84 percent say men often seem not to really hear.

3. 79 percent report painful and infuriating attitudes on the part of men in their love relationships.

4. 78 percent say ruefully that still, all too often in love relationships they have to fight for their rights and respect.

5. 76 percent state that their husband or lover rarely tries to draw them out or get them to speak about their thoughts and feelings the way women do (or try to do) for men.

6. 74 percent feel they lack "credibility" with the men they love.

7. 71 percent in long marriages had originally tried to draw their husbands out but finally gave up.

8. 71 percent say the men in their lives are afraid of emotion.

9. 69 percent of married women and 47 percent of single women say they have decided they do not like, or no longer trust, being "in love"; it is too volatile, too dangerous.

10. 63 percent meet with great resistance when they try to push their husband or lover to talk about feelings.

11. 59 percent believe passionate love cannot last.

12. 54 percent note stability as their reason for preferring loving, caring feelings over being passionately in love.

13. 52 percent doubt that men have a true desire for deeper communication.

14. 41 percent refuse to make a separation between "lust" and being "in love," feeling this is all part of one larger emotion.

15. 17 percent do not take being "in love" seriously; they say it represents an unbalanced mental state.

16. 17 percent say the communication in their relationship is good, makes them happy, adds to their life.

17. 10 percent describe real and equal emotional relationships with the men.

Almost any psychiatric practice could have produced this same chorus of complaints, but few clinicians have the literary talent or devotion to the topic to have organized it as well as Shere Hite.

However, what Hite did, and what so many other authors and commentators on these matters do, is leave the idea of love, the meaning of love, the complexity of love, to their respondents to decide. The result is 4,500 different opinions about what love is or means to each respondent.

In a Parisian patisserie one could say, "I'll take one of those things over there" and be rewarded with the éclair of choice. In a scholastic Latin competition one might write "res" for the general's briefcase and be only half wrong, because "res" can be used for almost anything for which we don't have another proper designation. When we are talking about love, though, surely we must do better. We must have more than one simple-word label for the many moments of human intercourse that describe those caring, wishing, and sexing times and events. We probably don't need 4,500 different words so that each respondent can tell her unique interpersonal "love transactions," but the likelihood that any two of them are talking about the same thing when they are talking about their "love life" is remote.

In this and Chapter 8, the love chapter, I shall try to remedy this. It is my contention that the way individuals understand relationships to those special other people whom they say they love deserves a more careful scrutiny. I also submit that a consequence of that scrutiny will be the realization that those transactions have been misnamed as love when that was not the case at all. As soon as this is realized, the grief for its loss will be far less traumatic.

It will be seen that only the magic of a word has been lost, not the fact of a true love relationship. Correction of this simple error of naming will give a new perspective on the feelings of frustration and bitterness. Since it wasn't love, why be so distraught?

I submit that the responders, and most of us in similar circumstances, are not talking about love. They are talking about neurotic self-destructive connections to the wrong partners for the wrong reasons. Lost in a realm of illusion and delusion, they have appealed to the magic of words for rescue. Oh, would that it were that easy. If only the words alone produced and effected true love. But it does not. Love in those cases is more often a "wish" word than an "is" word.

This book begins where Shere Hite's leaves off. It provides guidance through the maelstrom of interpersonal confusion which results from this love-word ambiguity. It shows that talk about loving and not loving has become more a word game than a reliable designation for this very complicated human relationship.

It is not the intent of this chapter to demean the substantial angst of those respondents so eloquently revealed and poetically systematized and chronicled in Hite's careful study. Each of these ladies conveyed important data, but the words they were using had no validity. While they were quite often naming the same experience, it never qualified for a true definition of love.

Hite did ask, "Are you in love? How can you tell? How would you define love? Is love the thing you work at in a relationship over a period of time? Is it the strong feelings you feel right now from the beginning for no known reason?" She did not follow through, however. She did not then correlate those answers to the other 125 answers provided by those same women. She and her respondents kept using the word "love" when talking about almost anything that had been going on between them and their partners. I hesitate to even say friends. A striking example of this is the definition of love given by one of my patients—"Of course I love him," she protested, "do you think I would put up with his shit if I didn't!"

As this chapter and the next will clarify, there love was the wrong word. All the conclusions that follow from such false naming are doomed to be false and dangerous. Hite revealed what no author has yet done as well or as completely, a narrative of the travesty of the love word game. These were not love relationships. They were neurotic connections. When you see this simple truth, all of her conclusions and the statistical assessment of them crumble.

Hite's book has nevertheless accomplished a great service. It tells better than any other thus far what is really going on between men and women. Her only mistake was that she accepted their language and syntax as if the women were in "love" relationships. This was a very dangerous error. Love can be a dangerous word, a word which confuses and then rationalizes the terrible things that go on between men and women in its name. Therefore, our first piece of business in this "unhitching from bitching" journey is to void the word "love" from such a profane and misplaced usage.

This habit of using a word to comfort ourselves into believing we understand something which we may not is not unique to the word "love." For example, there are a lot of things I do not know about the universe, but if I just say "that's God's way," my curiosity would be satisfied at least until a better answer comes along or until the premise in my belief in God's omniscience is disproved. Likewise, there are a lot of things we don't know about the interpersonal space, especially that powerful attachment between men and women. However, if and when we call it "love," we often feel better, albeit only briefly.

Perhaps this point can be clarified by relating it to a more physical event. We have all seen that apples fall from trees, but we didn't know much about the whys and wherefores of it until Sir Isaac Newton, from that mysterious space of doubt, wonder and genius, saw the gravity equations. Replacing mystery with numbers and then with meaning, he discovered from a manifestly simple existence a profound essence. I view this as my task and your opportunity with a reexamination of your love relationships.

Neither Shere Hite nor I know what is actually going on in the yoking together that characterizes so many interpersonal relationships called "love." However, as long as her respondents, whom I take to be representative of both men and women in general, and she as their spokesperson squeeze their agony into stories about whose love for whom is faulted, they will be missing the boat!

You can't get there from here. You can't get to better relationships between men and women by using a misunderstood, seldom studied and clearly outdated "love" word as your ticket or entitlement. It doesn't fit. The data is too complicated. We can't get all that stuff into a carry-on relationship.

Hite's book and others of its ilk have encouraged thousands of readers to seek asylum in derivatives of false premises about them and their interpersonal relationships. However, the success of those books has created an opportunity for me to counter-argue that as long as men and women do not know how to get their interpersonal connections properly labeled, they will not have good relationships with one another.

Remedial Step 1: We don't love them.

Remedial Step 2: They don't love us.

Why? Because we don't have a consensual validation or agreement on what love is. Why? Because we haven't thought it through very carefully. We don't know if it's an idea, a feeling, or a feeling about an idea, or an idea about a feeling. We don't know how to go from saying it to proving it. We don't know how to really know if they really mean it or if they're just saying it.

What most men do know, however, is that the trade-off of permanent or rehabilitative alimony seems like an unfair exchange for not loving someone any more or any longer. No guy that I know wants to trade his tomorrows after love cools for the small print in today's "I love you" agreements. Nor should any modern woman be so passively prone to repeat her daddy's little girl past for a word.

Shere Hite's book, while most often purporting to give testimony to what's wrong with men, has also revealed what's wrong with women. (Men, of course, are not innocents. They are as limited, frightened, and confused as their poorly prepared lady partners.) The conclusion: losers playing losers in the love game will both lose!

Surely any woman journalist, philosopher or psychologist has the right to render her assessment of women's goals, wishes and ambitions. But what are women's, or for that matter men's, entitlements to such fulfillments in their relationships? By what authority do we, as adults, know what any other adult should or must be doing better with or for us. Yet as soon as anyone says to anyone that they love them, oh how many debts and rules fill the void of that uncertainty. It is amazing that we are so ignorant on the Monday before love and so sure on the Tuesday after of what we must now do with one another: how we each must now behave!

Frankly, most of us don't know any more about love after than before we say we are in love. We just act as if we do, and there is no shortage of partners who will join us on that stage! But most of all, we act as if we now know what they must do as a consequence of their loving us.

Reading Shere Hite's book was an eye-opening experience for this psychiatrist. As docudrama of only a half-truth, her respondents are 100% right; i.e., that's exactly how they see it. They mean what they say. They are not wrong. They are only half-right! They clearly do not understand the other half-right elements of the real life equations in which they transact business with men. But, and here's the rub, neither do their male partners. Those men are also floundering guppies in the same semantic surf of "love means anything you wish it did depending on which day you say it!" It needs no test of its truth—just say it and it is true, and its consequences of your entitlement will follow. Terribly tragic consequences have been wrought upon the lives of those who play by the words and not by meanings. What sustains them is that their positions are consensus misapprehensions by either their consciousness-raising sisters or their bowling buddies. However, love's truth for either sex cannot be voted in by a majority of those polled.

Men or women in dysfunctional relationships will, of course, almost always blame their partners. After all, who is courageous enough in such a moment to say, "I'm so confused by my own insecurity; so lame, and maimed by the inequities of the social structure which has misnamed if not cursed me that I am a lame runner in the love race, and my relationships with others are diminished by the inadequacies which I endure. Anger, martyrdom, masochism and sexual confusion haunt my presence as harpies of an unresolved past where messages were double and what they (the folks that raised me) said wasn't the way it really was. "Such a character is a rare bird, and most folks will resort to blaming. To the blamers, though, know that you can't get self-awareness by paranoid projection. You've got to start at home plate. So come with me to the "unhitching from bitching" post.

Begin by letting go of the illusions that the men or womenfolks in your life should, could or must think, behave or feel differently than they do about you or anything else. Accept, at least for now, that "folks will be folks." For those who have attended (or have had a spouse or live-in attend) an EST seminar, you know that their cryptic way of delivering this same message is "What is, is!"

Perhaps I should place a caveat here so that no reader will believe that I do not appreciate how invidious the politically male-dominated system of prejudice against women has been. However, what is or was "rotten in Denmark" in terms of political, educational, religious and vocational male-chauvinistic-pig prejudice and dominance is not on my agenda for remedy. The fact is that it is now possible (probably for the first time in the history of Western society) for young men and women to joust fairly in the love game. Furthermore, older men and women are reentering this arena after their children have gone and they are "one spouse down" and anxious to try again.

Having accepted for now that folks will be folks, appreciate that your inspiration, your good advice and your needs need not prevail. They are like placebos for psychoneurosis. They will produce only a brief respite in the turmoil of your relationships. They will allow you merely to retreat to a neutral corner, Changing others by threat or by tears will only transiently reduce the volume in the "poor me" sonata. It will not change the beat or the melody.

Get on with the business of being yourself. Give your partner a new context of you in which the old neurotic tradeoffs no longer balance. Let them remain their "perfect" (though incompatible) selves with you. Yes, "perfect." Before you recoil, though, please read on! That is not to say they have achieved an ideal perfection or actualization of their existence or that they have perfect essence. It means they are perfect who they are and so are you a perfect you. It also does not mean they cannot change. It means that what you see is what you got and it is only what it is. Thus, they have their perfect "is-ness" and so do you.

Perfect does not mean perfect in comparison to others, but in its rareness and exclusivity. It means one of a kind. A perfect Van Gogh is no more perfect than a perfect Schwartz. It is just that one is the work of an artistic genius and one is the winner in a fifth grade art contest. But they are both perfect what they are!

An old baseball story about three umpires may make this point a bit clearer. Comparing notes on how to determine what is a strike, one says, "I call 'em as I see 'em!" The other says, "I calls them as they are." The third says, "They ain't nothin' 'til I calls 'em."

Which umpire are you in the love game? This book will help you become the second. Call them as they are and let yourself be called as you are, and take heart from the knowledge that love, in order to be, derives from the virtue of the lover. It can be measured and it must be deserved!

8

The Facts of Love

While children and adolescents can play infatuation, sex and child-love games, only adults can "adult-love" each other. So let's begin by determining what are the necessary and essential elements which go into validating the presence of "adult-love." But before we do that, let's assert that its primary property is that its presence can be validated and its truth can be measured.

"Adult-love" is an interpersonal transaction only possible between those intelligent and mature enough to comprehend its meaning and consequences. Yes, you heard me correctly, only adults can love adults. Only adults have a sense of the "I" who "lives" in the body and, through the nurturing experiences of language, empathy and caring, has had his or her carnal nature so tamed and refined, so acculturated and personified by bonding to significant others, that such love derivatives as endearment, devotion and self-sacrifice may now occur. With this definition we establish it as an interpersonal transaction, rather than an interobject or interbody or intrapersonal experience, thus denying the distortion that bodies make love to other bodies, or have love for other bodies.

What I am suggesting here is nothing more complicated than applying, to the love protest, those same logical demands that one places upon most other communications of prowess, ability, virtue or intent. "Adult-love" is provable. One's entitlement to utter it should be testable and measurable. An adult lover should have to demonstrate the psychological dexterity and emotional discipline to qualify for membership in the "Can Love Society."

Although adult-love does begin as a here and now transaction, its future thrust defines its true worth and allows it to convey a message that no other properly used word can. Adult-love is an idea which embodies not only the continuity of selves in time, but the ability to keep agreements in the future that are promised in the present. It connects us to our future and our posterity. It describes a "becoming together agreement," and it requires that the players are sensitive, mature and intelligent enough to comprehend these concepts. While bodies "loving" bodies has been properly compared to masturbation with objects, or fetishistic perversion, adult-love is never unipolar or unilateral. It always involves two whole individuals in dialogue and dialove with each other. Such a synthesis, however, is not fusion. The lines of cleavage stay. I am still OK alone, but I am more with you. I complement, but do not compromise, you. I extend you. I am with you in the real world where our real selves can touch and share, where agreements can be kept, where promises are sacred, where error is forgiven, where healing follows injury and where the joy of "us" may prevail over either of our separate satisfactions.

This state of togetherness has many of the characteristics of a political state. It accepts laws and sanctions to secure its ethical contracts, and assigns privileges and rights to the contract signatories. Love, I submit, is a functional derivative of personal ethics, and is not antithetical to reason or logic.

Understanding and acquiescing to the ethical posture of those with whom we seek to find love, not just described or spoken, but lived in their daily lives, is unmatched for reliability as a determinant for achieving an adult-love relationship. Therefore, those who cannot reason love's elements nor comprehend its ethics and keep its promises, are by definition incapable of asserting its presence. Since appreciation of these elements lies beyond the will, talent, wit and intelligence of children by this very definition, the love option is not possible for them or for their adult immature equivalents.

At first it may sound Scrooge-like to say that children are, by this definition, disenfranchised from the love contract, but I believe its merit will soon become apparent. Just as it is proper to have a separate censuring system for children, or for mentally or emotionally immature adults who violate society's rules and trespass against its sanctions, so must we stand watch at the gates of union where such persons connect and disallow their playing adult games with only alphabet blocks.

As long as we aspire to a system in which love is the entree to, and the guiding principle of, marriage, and as long as we continue to view the family as the unit to which we consign the civilizing process, we must secure a system in which those who request society's permission to have such a responsibility pass some test of eligibility—since loving is such a serious and complex contract—emotionally or mentally immature or deficient persons cannot be expected to ahere to its conditions.

So, how do we find reasonably responsible people, and how do we take the measure of their abilities to love? Only by noting how securely they hold their allegiance to the truth and how reliably they adhere to facts and logic. Only by observing their understanding of territorial rights and imperatives. Only by seeing their sense of mercy and forgiveness. Only by watching how much they charge for favors and how they punish for error. Only by examining their respect for their neighbor's body, property and sacred symbols. For only by recording these crucial items, on all those whom we aspire to love or who invite us to accept their loving, can we truly know that love exists in our relationship. I am reminded of a beach walk with a friend of mine some years ago and commenting to him upon the success of his love/marriage life which was so apparent to me as his house guest that weekend. "You know, Al," he replied, "it's really quite simple. From the minute I get up in the morning to the time I go to sleep at night, I am constantly trying to figure out and behave in a way that pleases my wife." Before I could interrupt with my reply, to what appeared to be a somewhat oversimple, if not Pollyannaish formula, he continued "… and can you believe this, Al, she feels exactly the same way about me."

Contrast this with another incident of a discussion also overheard recently between two friends, one an interior designer, the other a colleague psychiatrist. "If you don't mind, Doc" the second fellow spoke, "I'd like to tell you what I think is wrong with your relationship to your wife" (having just had lunch with his doctor friend and his wife). "Sure," he replied, "what?" The reply: "You answer her when she speaks!"

I offer these anecdotes not to pronounce that the first couple is an example of what love is, and the second an example of what love ain't, but to emphasize that the way folks actually behave with one another is where the measure can be taken of whether they are in love.

Furthermore, because the love equation must be balanced, it is necessary to consider the experiences of receiving, as well as conveying, the adult-love message. For just as only adults can legitimately deliver the adult-love message, so can only mature adults encode and validate adult-love's worth and meaning. This truth further diminishes the opportunity for already disenfranchised children and immature imposters from playing the adult-love game. Adult-love can only be exchanged by mature, rational partners. You must be an advanced player in the game of human intercourse to either adult-love or validate another's adult-love for you. Adult-love *matches* are of course between those who can do both. However, because you love another and he or she can validate its worth, it does not necessarily follow that you in turn will be loved. Any two players with minimal language skills can murmur or exclaim "I love you," but the words "I love you" have no intrinsic value. As Eliza Doolittle so clearly stated to her Henry Higgins "if you're in love, *show me!*" Adult-love requires these two reagents of authentication: (1) proof that the givers are adult-love capable, (2) proof that the receivers are adult-love literate and deserving.

To believe this is not so betrays two wishes, (1) a return to that regressed state of our infantile and juvenile past, when our very presence in the life of our own parents qualified us for the bounty of their giving and sacrifice for us, and (2) a return to that dangerous equation which states because you make my body feel so good, I must love you or, worse than that, you must love me! We must learn a new language game which destigmatizes mutual masturbation and allows non-adult-loving sexual intercourse to be more acceptably labeled, while ridding it entirely from the misnomer of lovemaking.

As a matter of fact, in these days of AIDS awareness and safe sex, there has never been a more timely occasion to develop this far more appropriate appreciation of the fact that genital intercourse is often just one of several mechanisms of mutual masturbation, and that there are much safer and more reliable forms of achieving not only sexual pleasure but orgasm, with many other techniques. However, whichever way Joe and Nancy decide to have sexual fun, let them be further relieved of the shibboleth that because they "did it," they must have "loved one another," or that because they "love one another" it's OK to "do it."

Some further thoughts now on loveableness. Most of us were initially cared for without challenge or responsibility to deserve it. It was our "thereness" and the other's motive to deliver the caring that made that transaction work. All we had to do was be there and our extrauterine needs would be served with the same devotion and immediacy as our intrauterine needs. If this chapter has done nothing more than rename that transaction as "child-loving," it has taken a megastep forward in expanding your appreciation for the vast differences between such a transaction and adult-loving.

More simply stated, in "child-loving," the child-lover has accepted the task and responsibilities of nurturing another. The child-lover gives and the child-loved receives. On some cherished day when the receiver has achieved primitive language skills, the child-lover may hear, "I love you, too." However, what is that love, other than a statement of appreciation? The equation reads: when someone does all that good stuff for me and says he/she loves me, I say I love him/her too. Surely this is not the adult-love we adults are looking for in our post-adolescent years. Furthermore, though all child-loving parents soon discover tickling, kissing and caressing their children gives them pleasure, few will feel comfortable in calling those "sexual" encounters. But isn't this reluctance just another word-game problem?

I contend it is. If we would call such sexual stimulation by its right name, we would so destigmatize the word "sex" that adult–adult sexual intercourse would no longer need to be called "love-making." And, if masturbation still feels like a too-crass label, we could call it "child-loving" or "puppy-loving."

Though adult-love can be enhanced by sexual activities, giving or receiving sexual pleasure is not a subset of love nor a necessary or essential measure of its presence.

Adult-love is not for children, just as ethics are not for children, nor is marriage! Maybe we can't stop teen pregnancy, but we can stop child marriage, if we finally realize these crucial distinctions between adult-love and child-love. Who wins when the state is enjoined to bless a union of child-lovers and anoint its participants as if they knew what they were agreeing to?

As a psychiatrist I am regularly called upon to help determine whether members of Florida's geriatric community are competent to disburse their bounty by will, or determine where or how they shall die. Is it so preposterous to wonder whether some test of entitlement is in order, to determine who can appreciate the nature and complexity of the laws of marriage and divorce, or the responsibilities of having and raising children? Though legislating a competence statute to determine eligibility for marriage may be too radical for our society at this time, it would certainly help if our culture disdained "child-love marriages" with the same certainty it now does for adult–child sexuality.

A true appreciation of the concepts propounded here disallows the act of sexual intercourse from ever again being called "love making." The trade-off may be no more complex than finding a nicer, more tender and endearing word than "fornication," for sexual relations between caring but not loving partners.

Indeed, I have often wondered whether those polar extremes of language—"loving" and "fucking"—are rooted in a primitive, if not satanic, formula imposed upon the less well-informed by the keepers of the grail, such that to serve their needs, sexual congress between the masses would be either gross and obscene or sanctified and blessed, thereby consigning its participants into the sacrament of marriage or the caverns of degradation. How otherwise can we explain that no intermediary words or ideas are commonly used to describe the vast, interpersonal, territorial space between these two extremes? Because of this semantic no-man and no-woman's world, the word love, as it is commonly used today, deceives more often than conveys the genuine presence of a complex idea. Rather it conveys in today's vernacular a more magical than real message. And when not magical, love, inappropriately, has been co-opted as a designation for a religious, rather than an interpersonal, experience. This connection to religion, in my judgment, also requires emergency re-evaluation. You see, whether God is or is not "love" may be a relevant topic for theological debate but it should have little to do with Ken telling Barbie on prom night that he loves her. Insisting otherwise is a folly which has been known to produce tragic consequences, i.e.,"Hello, Mrs. Jones, this is Jake Jarrell, Martha's dad. I think we need to get together and talk about what we're going to do about the new soul which our children have created."

Not understanding the love language-world in which we live is as dangerous, if not more so, than not understanding our physical world. "Sally, be careful! That fire is hot and you can burn yourself." "Charlie, come down off that roof! If you fall, you'll break your neck." Yes, most parents get fair to good marks on teaching their children about physical dangers. But how do they teach them about what love is? The answer is—they don't. Why? Because as often as not they themselves don't know what love is!

More importantly, they have not modeled it. Most parents exhibit the same, fixed, juvenile, unconscious ideas about love as those just described. These simplistic ideas have become so deeply imbedded in the unconscious, and have secured such primacy over our behavior, that to rethink them has become almost blasphemy.

This is well-illustrated by William James's classic principles of psychology which he wrote in 1890, and which served, with minimal revision, as the primary college text of psychology for almost the next fifty years. James devoted only two pages to love.

Almost one hundred years later, Masters and Johnson, in their 564-page book *Sex and Loving*, have devoted twenty pages (only three and one-half percent of their text) to love, despite including it in their title. Why, I wonder, did the publisher, a superbly reputable house, seduce the buyer who customarily doesn't review the Table of Contents, into believing the book is about sex and human loving? Perhaps because that's all the authors know about love. Perhaps just three and one-half percent of their understanding of sex and human loving is about loving, and ninety-six and one-half percent is about sex. And if that's all the experts know, what can we just plain folks be expected to know about what love actually is? Perhaps it is because love, like gravity, is dismissed by most folks as another event which controls our lives but just can't be fathomed by the average observer? But love can be understood and its counterfeiters can be exposed!

Begin by realizing that love is not what, to this very moment, you have believed it to be, thought it to be, felt it to be.

If we were talking about snowflakes or potatoes, in cultures in which snow or potatoes were important, we would probably have a dozen words to distinguish among their various types, configurations or subsets. For some reason, however, in our society there is only the love word for that vast complex of feelings, ideas and emotions about the interpersonal transactions of caring adults. Surely that is not a happenstance. It is a cultural retreat, an expedient, fashioned by the culture mongers and power brokers who prefer that it is better if folks remain mired in such ambiguity, rather than be encouraged to apply the same logic to their personal life that they provide to the physical and financial world. Thus we are compelled to look to authority and religion for rituals, rather than logical formulas, for determining how we bond ourselves to significant other people and how we create families. These priests and governors have wrested from us the opportunity of making our intimate connections on a rational and reliable basis. This chapter of this book protests that this preposterous status quo must go. It is my contention that love's presence must conform to the laws of logic. That cannot be a fact of love which is not a fact!

That which is not love cannot be made love by pronouncement. In the blasphemous name of love, the worst atrocities in the history of mankind have been committed. However, I shall leave such global issues for others to reflect upon. I simply want my readers to understand their love lives and inspire them to make ideational adjustments. By so doing you may discover this option for leaving the bitching box, namely that it wasn't their love that ticketed you in, nor is it love that sustains your continuing presence there. As soon as you realize this, it becomes so much easier to end a bitching relationship.

9

What about Therapy?

In my practice, I tell patients that relationships which cannot be seen are obscene. By that I mean that relations that cannot be observed, cannot be questioned, cannot be touched for fear of shattering, cannot be considered for fear of exploding, are often bitching contests which are not only psychologically but physically dangerous.

While one of the bitching partners may be available to relate the particulars of the disharmonious union, seldom in true bitching relationships do the two parties come to a therapist together for an honest look at "their" relationship. Also, it cannot be presumed that the partner who does come in for help is the one with the more serious problems. There is, of course, a valid rationale for being apprehensive about having your relationship to another scrutinized, and in the early hours, "letting it all hang out" would be a serious error. Therefore, I encourage my couple patients to let their ears hang out and their tongues hang in during the early hours of therapy. By the time most couples seek help, screaming has replaced listening and they have each heard what they scream a hundred times before. What is quickly learned in therapy, however, is that they have never heard what somebody else hears, especially with the trained ears of a good counselor.

Happily, people can and do change, and many troubled couples can resolve their problems. Yet in order to do this, they must have the courage to endure the pain of changing, which often is initially more severe than the pain of maintaining the status quo. This is where a good therapist fits in. The therapist helps balance those pain equations. He or she will stay with you both until the fever of distortion breaks, until the time when the pain of "that's mine, give it back to me," converts to "this is ours—and this is how it must be shared."

If sharing is the name of the game, then we need to take a look at the time and place where it first occurred, i.e., the Oedipal place and Electra time. We all started from that triangle—Dad, Mom (or their equivalents), and ourselves—to achieve our oneness. Winnicott called this oneness "learning to be alone with others," and Bowlby and Storr have written scholarly treatises about its variations.

The issue, however, endures as an ultimately simple one. Our unity, our separate wholeness, turns on how well or how poorly we initially connected to those parental two and whether we left them through chaos or tragedy for our independence, or with their blessings and a packed lunch.

Is it any wonder, then, that the troubled couple may have to return to another triangle, i.e., the helping other to find themselves again, or maybe for the very first time?

What we soon learn as therapists of these relationships is that they are not "being with" relationships, but "having you" relationships.

This, of course, accounts for the panic when each considers losing their partners.

A few pages from Ernest Becker's book, *The Denial of Death*, should help you understand this a bit better. He explained how we impoverish and dilute our time of living by not placing it in the gestalt of our dying. May I suggest that we likewise demean and diminish our relationships if we don't properly put them in the gestalt of their ending.

Indeed, this is the critical variable of possibility where those in bitching relationships are too timid to see.

I am convinced that if we don't play in a minor key every day of our lives this libretto: "What you have today, you may not have tomorrow," be it your life or your love, you will never properly savor the tones, sights and smells of your present!

Good relationships allow separate whole others to be dieable and thus more livable. Failure to accept the inevitability of loss by fate, will, or idiosyncrasy, is a self-destructive delusion! We should only want someone who can bear to be without us, though they may prefer not to be. And we should, of course, be that person ourselves. We should be able to say that very same thing to them. We should want someone who would not emotionally bleed to death from the wound of our separation from them. Contrary to the junk of romance novels, "needing you" and "must have you" and "can't live without you" are not more profound representations of caring than "I would very much like to be with you, but I am whole without you."

My remedy for this problem for my patients begins with a psychobiography with this special focus. Look back for anger. Look back into your growth and developmental years, inventory the nature and extent of your relationships to those special others who gave you your name. See how you bonded to each of them. Learn how tenaciously you held to their actual presence, and how you yearned for them in their absence. How frightened of aloneness were you then, and most importantly, did you savor the great gift of "being along with them"— knowing they were there, but being separate and safe in your "own room"?

Compare this to how alone you feel now with the threat of the dissolution of your union to a current partner. How much fear, anger, and retaliation does this threat of loss provoke at them? My therapy then pursues the answers to these questions. Do they know where this anger came from? Do they have any idea how to dissipate it? Do they seek revenge, death, pain or destruction of you as the disappointing partner? Do they permit forgiveness? Do they foresee peace on the other side of the chaos of loss? Do they see other interpersonal continents to be explored and new rivers of friendship to cross? Or are they abandoned and without hope? As folks consider the answers to these questions, I note how feelings of anger, disappointment, rage and confusion attach to their ideas of betrayal, entitlement and retribution. I then ask them to consider, perhaps for the first time in their lives, how and at what crucial moments in their growth and development ideas such as these first attached themselves to those feelings. I hope this book can serve that very purpose for my readers as well.

Though we all know how loss feels, what we think about it is even more critical! The fact is that feelings can be understood by neurochemists as physical expressions of simple chemical reactions, i.e., delayed serotonin uptake reducing sexual libido, or estrogen–progesterone imbalance altering the mood of the premenstrual housewife. Therefore, for these feelings, a physician therapist may provide a remedy by prescribing tranquilizers or antidepressants without psycho-analytic understanding of underlying psychological causation or dynamics.

Psychologists and psychiatrists, on the other hand, seek to understand the ideas or hypotheses which attend these feelings. However, they often disagree upon which theory is correct. Freudians may explain the feelings of loss according to ideas of castration. Adlerians may explain them as loss of power. Theologians may explain them as crosses to bear in God's plan. Each then applies his or her unique set of balancing or neutralizing ideas to replace those which are, if not causing, at least contributing to the problems. This is referred to as insight.

Even without such intervention, however, each of us, without benefit or liability of a formal theory of personality, has our own Rosetta Stone. We know what meaning we give to the behavior of others, what responses we should make to our feelings, and what formulas we must use to explain their presence. What we far too often cannot do, however, is control our feelings. And just as importantly, most of us seldom question the enduring veracity or worth of our explanations or hypotheses on what facts deserve what feelings.

This book is intended to demonstrate that education and psychotherapy are our tickets to a progressive alteration of our limited capacity in this regard. As the Hebrew scholars taught in their elegiac Yom Kippur chant that penitence, prayer and charity could avert God's decree of punishment for yesterday's sins, so have we in psychiatry learned that forgiveness, open-mindedness and humility can permit space for deleting or editing the emotional and ideational debris which clutters our paths to self-actualization and keeps us as knee-jerking anatomical preparations.

Since ideas are made of words manufactured by that most sophisticated computer, the brain, they cannot defy computer logic; i.e., garbage in, garbage out. Our task is to find the garbage of your guilt and find its proper exit route. One predominantly "garbaceous" idea is that you are more responsible for the status quo needs of your partner in a crazy relationship then you are for your own sanity.

A critical method for accomplishing this in my practice, and the thesis of this text for people in general, is to resolve the confusion between feelings and ideas! Scrutinize not only such classic feelings as love and guilt, but wherever feelings and ideas coexist. It is an enduring truth of my practice that the feelings of bitching partners almost always coexist with distorted ideas.

Let me now put this point into historical context. Our earliest understanding of the human psyche as revealed in Freudian psychology taught that primitive instinct, hidden in the unconscious mind, was contained from discovery and expression by society's sanctions against such unbridled energy. At the site of collision when the forces were not balanced, anxiety emerged as the discontent of our civilization.

At the beginning of my psychiatric residency, there was an intellectual rush that accompanied my awareness of the power and complexity of those unconscious erotic and aggressive forces in my patients and the network of defensive mechanisms created to thwart their direct expression. Early therapy techniques relied on the release of repression with its accompanying catharsis for treatment. But many patients remained impaired and still anxious and mentally troubled.

These clinical failures stimulated the psychoanalysts to explore another form of anxiety which was located, not at the interface between primitive wishes and society's restraints, but at the interface between our demands upon ourselves to be ideal and the frustrations of not living up to those standards.

This anxiety is called superego anxiety, and it is explained as follows: Somewhere in our developmental lives, as part of the civilizing process, we incorporated into our psyche crucial formulas about right and wrong, and good and bad, in the process of learning what did or did not please our parents or protectors. The motivation factor for learning these values was not only the pleasure of securing their approval but the avoidance of pain and punishment for disobedience to their wishes. Then two simple processes, incorporation and internalization, made it possible for us to punish ourselves if we did, said or thought what was prohibited by them!

Thus was born our ego ideal, an internal image of our best selves, a set of ideas about ourselves which, if expressed in the real world, would produce an ideal person, a person with the right set of ideas and the behaviors to match. If not expressed or held, however, a bad child would be produced who should be scolded and punished.

Superego anxiety became the downside of this equation. For with this internalization, not only are we vulnerable to the anxiety which occurs when wish meets external restraint, but internal restraint as well. When "don't wet the bed, don't touch Daddy's papers, don't hit you sister" took this gigantic leap of internalization "for if you do, you will not only by punished by a watchful real world adult, but by yourself as well," guilt was born!

Self against self is "I didn't do what I was supposed to do. I'm not the person I should be." This is the guilt which bitching partners project upon their mates to avoid at almost all costs the awareness of their own limitations. By understanding this process we see that where civilization has prevailed and nurture has triumphed over nature, patients in particular, and all of us in general, are left with the discontents of anxiety and guilt. Libido can be constrained first by force of others, and then by the others. Psychoanalysts of all theoretical persuasions have recently become as interested in the nature and mechanism of this superego anxiety by failing to achieve our ego ideals as they have been in their initial quest for the raw libido itself.

Now listen to this terrifying expansion of this phenomenon which initially transformed real parents or authorities into internal ones. Almost any idea which they held about almost anything can also be incorporated into us and made critical to our existence. We are thereby rendered anxiety-prone when we do not live up to even the most ridiculously minor element of their plan for us. We can get the same high levels of anxiety or guilt in failure to adhere to any ideas which we have absorbed into our superego, not just the big biblical ones.

While some may only experience this anxiety in violation of the most basic taboos of the culture, some folks can experience it over trivia. Any trivial parental bias can become the nemesis of the prone child who fears not only not doing what Daddy says he shouldn't do, but thinking or believing what Daddy says he shouldn't think or believe about almost anything.

This next event is the most frightening of all. We can project that same hostility against ourselves against others when they trespass against those same rules or ideas, i.e., not only will I punish myself if I don't comport with the wishes of my authorities, but I will punish you if you don't!

Look no further than the recent death sentence which was brought down upon the house of Salman Rushdie for his novel *Satanic Verses* by a nation of believers in the idea that his blasphemy justifies homicide, to emphasize this point. In fact, blasphemy provides an almost perfect reference for this point because it is an idea, not an act. It is not a "sticks and stones" crime, but a word crime.

But unnaming can avert the evil decree! That is the process which all the psychotherapies endeavor to accomplish, the renaming of the self modifying yesterday's ego ideal to become today's ego real! This transformation of values on the issues of love is addressed in the chapter on love, herein. It is uniquely critical to the unhitching from bitching process, but is relevant across the board of all interpersonal values and prejudgments.

On the occasion of my first convocation at Brown University, I was awed by the stature and rhetoric of then University President and Speech Writer for President Eisenhower, Henry Merrit Wriston.

"Here," he proclaimed, "you will make the acquaintance of great ideas." And so I did, and found this to be the greatest idea of them all, i.e., the magic and the power of ideas themselves. Words over passion. Concept over chaos. Knowledge over ignorance. Insight over neurosis. This is the ultimate triumph of where id was, therefore shall ego be, now extended to become where false ideal was there shall timely reality now reside.

What I have also sadly come to appreciate from that search for explanations to replace ignorance, answers to satisfy questions, news to replace the uncertain, and reality to replace the neurotic and psychotic distortion, is that while knowledge may set you free, pseudo-knowledge will lock you up. It will abort your actualization. It will cripple your nimble limbs.

False ideas can be implanted into your innocent prepubescent brain during the earliest hours of your growth and development and can dominate your entire adult life. As the King of Siam so aptly put it, "You've got to be taught to hate." We are not only forever vulnerable to the eruptions of our most primitive and primordial instinctual energies, but to the transformation of those energies into Husseiniac- and Khomeiniac-psychotic ideas propounded in the names of Allah, Beta, Yahwah, or Adolf. We folks—all of us—are prejudice-prone, and no new thought can insinuate itself into our bias nor new idea germinate from our cortex until we are relieved of those already fixed in place.

Another Elvin Semrad story demonstrates the place of ideational rigidity in our lives. He likened us residents in his didactic group to a crowd of porcupines on an especially cold winter morning. "Sure," proclaimed one porcupine, "we could cluster together and share the warmth." "But what about the damned spines?" inquired another. In the interpersonal arena, there is of course, warmth to be shared, and spines to be folded—and many are made of ideas!

Consider these examples taken from my random group therapy sessions. Observe how vehemently people will attack the most banal acts or statements of their groupmates in the name of an idea but hardly an ideal: "If you don't stop folding that napkin, John, I will break your fingers"—or "I haven't liked you, Teresa, since you first showed up. There's just something about you!"

What's going on here anyway? Why do those folks connect so dramatically to such manifest trivia in their lives? The answer, of course, is that it is not trivial to them, and as they often exclaim, "I have a right to my feelings!" Maybe they do, but so do we have a right to know that they are the kind of guys who break the fingers of those who nervously fold napkins, or at least want to break them! For those who are learning of this phenomenon for the first time, I know it sounds silly. But perhaps the following, more dramatic example from my practice will convince you that although it sounds silly, it has pathetically serious consequences.

Sarah, a teenager, had taken a serious overdose of her mother's Valium and explains her behavior: "It's my life, isn't it? Anyway, do you know how many teenagers try to kill themselves every year?"

Choosing to not debate these arguments with counterpoints, I asked instead, "Sarah, do you think that if you were engaged to be married, that you would have a moral obligation to divulge your ideas about suicide to your fiancé?" I followed then with this related question: "Do you think that people who will unilaterally break their connections to other people should have their male or female 'tubes' tied?"

"You must be crazy," she replied. "Do you think people talk like that? Do you think I'm gonna say to my boyfriend—oh, by the way, when things get tough with me, I might try to kill myself if I feel like it? Or, I guess maybe I better have my tubes tied before we commit to having a family, because at least then it will be only one of you that I leave."

I answered, "No, Sarah, I don't think you would, but I wish you would."

I wish she and others wondered and worried about the ethics of their relationships, and by that I mean I wish they would become better students of the hidden broad agenda of the ethical ideas which govern their behavior.

While I do not expect that each of you shall all become mavens of your own unconscious, I do wish you knew more about the many unspoken quid pro quos of your existence, especially those that underlie your sense of entitlement and need to have others fit into stories for which only one of you has the next paragraph.

Listen to a lunatic murderer on some television documentary for your ultimate confrontation with this phenomenon. Hear how an entirely innocent farm family was drawn into his paranoid delusions and annihilated on the basis of a fanatic distortion of his and their reality. Realize that for every megafortress of psychotic paranoid delusional thinking, there are tens of thousands of mini-systems of aberrant beliefs and formulas in which we others are nothing more than the objects upon which projectionists cast their images of entitlement, random other players whom they meet on a casual daily basis. One arena in which this almost always occurs is the bitching box.

Some psychiatrists will argue quite cogently that the role of the long-suffering partner or protector is 50% of the total psychopathology of the bitching relationship. While I also believe that this formula has relevance, it is only correct after many months of sameness in such relationships. Long before then, there are the early warning signs of imminent bitching. A few examples follow:

1. Note who is the more aggressive or needful in the earliest hours of encounter for change, even if it is manifestly questing to go from good to better. These demands more often reveal the fraud of the preceding acceptances than genuine ambition for maturation of a relationship.

2. Look out for the slow erosion of the will of the one and the eroticizing of the will or whim of the other. This is revealed by the obstinate belief that only with this one person can one's sexuality be expressed in such a magnificent fashion, if at all.

3. Failures in communication; I shall tarry a bit longer on this one.

Carefully needlepointed into a plaque on my office waiting room wall is the Hebrew verse of Genesis III.9: "… and God came into the Garden of Eden and said, 'Adam, where are thou?'" Jewish scholars have identified this sentence as the earliest Biblical sanction for the belief that man has a right to a one-on-one connection with his creator.

Omniscient, omnipotent, and omnipresent, surely Yahweh knew where Adam was and what he had done. He had conspired with the snake and eaten the apple of knowledge. But God's reaction was unequivocally clear and prophetic. Rather than protesting, "Adam, I know where you are, and what you have done, and what my decision shall be for your punishment," he says, "Adam, where are you? Adam, talk to me. Adam, I have audience for your story, and by my audience I shall advance our union. For though punishment, pardon or reward shall follow, it shall be of our union, not from my authority alone." Man and God in dialogue, this was and endures as the ultimate prototype axis for the discovery first of our likeness to Him, and then of our love and likeness for each other which comes from this. For in the final analysis, is not God or any higher power just another way of giving more value to an idea than to our flesh?

Maybe that is what "God is Love" really means. Maybe "God's listening" is the measure of His love—and maybe it is the measure of ours, especially if listening means that I have room for your words and your ideas in my world. I know how to be with you. For this one fact is certain; in the bitching trap there is no listening. It has been replaced by "win or lose." In the bitching box, there are only two deaf I's in combat for the territory that can only be shared with compromise.

Left alone, there is no resolution. As long as they grip so tenaciously to each other's necks, they are too wide to go through the peace door. But their sentence is not eternal. Though good advice cannot crack the granite of their destructive union, and clearly falls on deaf and preoccupied ears, the very presence of a listening third person can make all the difference. For, though they do not need to be talked to, they need to be listened to by a significant third other. It will be then, and perhaps only then, that they can hear themselves.

This is the marvelous chapter of all the psychotherapies which are basically variations of the listening art, i.e., that devoted listening can fathom the primitive equations of patients, revealing the fallacies of their uninterrupted arguments. The scream of discovery, "Eureka! I do not own my own choices, I am spoken for, I am owned, I am possessed by those ill-bred mongrel dogs of fears." These are the true answers which emerge as their stories are heard by each of the players.

On the final page of *Portnoy's Complaint*, the psychiatrist says, "Now we can begin!" This beginning for Portnoy, I hope, can be yours as well. When your bitching story finally ends, you get one step closer to such powerful insights as "Yes, I am afraid of knowing me, afraid of not being same, afraid of not being sane, afraid of not being at all, afraid of letting go of my fixed ideas!"

Folks are locked into these sadomasochistic connections as if their very existence depended upon them, as if loss of the partner were plague upon their houses.

Remember also that bitching partners can endure seemingly forever, so if you're waiting for them to leave, forget it. They stay because it saves them from having to look elsewhere for the whys of their misery or having to consider their own limits. You are the object which protects, yes protects, them from the explosion of pain which follows aloneness with its self-awareness and self-doubts. Loss of you means loss of their ideas about themselves as well. Being with you is so much better than being alone with this paradox, and you are so easily replaced when you finally do leave. Why? Because you are not really you. You are what they need you to be and anyone can be that! Get it? You are just an object for their naming, you are clay for sculpting, a blank sheet of paper for their great American novel of the misunderstood "lover."

Wow! What a put-down! You are an anybody! You are just one of thousands of partners entwined in these absurd destructive duos, shackled by those deadly twins, sadism and masochism. Such sick and sad connections derive their staying power not from caring, love or respect, but fear, habit and compulsion. These partners choose the noise of someone's anger and disappointment to the silence of their own uncertainty. Their message is clear, they prefer the pain of you both than the truth of themselves alone.

They, of course, don't realize this. But you must! You must dare to know that you are not this wonderful person that their neurotic need has created!

This is not a lovers' quarrel. This is a bitching relationship, and as noted in Chapter 1, bitching is a neurotic process, rooted in unreal arguments. It is as unrealistic as phobia and obsession. It is defensive, it is antithetical to truth and loving, it is derived from false premise and thus destined to false conclusion. It is garbage in and garbage out. It is gamesmanship in which childhood fears and ploys govern responses. It is where simple giving and trust are foresworn and replaced by "gimme, gimme, gimme!" It's wanting what we want only when we want it. It's sandbox humor and unpractical joking.

But so often—oh so often—it wears the mask of love!

10

Goodbye and Rebirth

Well, you've finally done it, or it's been done to you, and here you are the next morning: alone. Perhaps for the first time in your life, you're a single adult!

What is a single adult? How does he live? What is his habitat? What are his ecosystems? Who are his prey and who are his predators? What do single folks do, anyway? Is it normal to be a single adult? If so, for how long? If you don't have or want a relationship with another person of the same or opposite sex for now or forever, does that mean you can't? Are you broken? Is this dust what you must bear until you do better by connecting to someone?

Look no further than Anthony Storr's recent best-selling book *Solitude* to discover the normalcy of solitude. Therefore, I will not tarry any longer with those questions. Yes, solitude and aloneness is normal and requires no apology. There is no American Psychiatric Association mental illness labeled "alone," although if there were, as so many other traits of human existence have been medicalized, it would probably be called *unifrenia*.

But the peace of aloneness cannot occur until you have been psychologically, as well as physically, disconnected from your recent partner. Therefore, this chapter is concerned with those mental bonds that still tie and those emotional shackles that daily remind you that you are still a psychological prisoner of attachment. Consequently, we shall come full circle to reinforce some earlier points about the love game, and will reaffirm the pervading aphorism, "As soon as you know it isn't love, it's easier, oh so much easier, to say goodbye!"

In the immediate aftermath of your unhitching from bitching, you will experience, paradoxically, not euphoria but guilt and her hand-maidens, loneliness and rationalization. Loss of a once cared for, if not loved, partner more often opens the door of self-depreciation than of feelings of emancipation. Surely you recognize these plaints of the bereaved:

Woe is me, bad is me!
I did something I should not have done!
I should have done something I didn't do!

I was not the person I should have been!
I am discovered to be the person I wish I weren't!

To understand this, we must recall several points made in Chapters 1 and 7, the "bitching" and "love" chapters. Remember how we belabored the differences between feelings and ideas? Here we are again with another variation of this same concern to reflect upon. Again, we must take note that guilt is not a feeling, it is an idea. Sadness and depression are feelings, hunger and thirst are feelings, anxiety and anger are feelings. That's why pharmacotherapists can talk scientifically about treating the likes of those symptoms with anxiolytics and antidepressants. No matter how, why or when these symptoms appear, once they are measured and assessed, they can be neurochemically neutralized. For guilt, though, there is no chemical solvent.

It must be thought out because we were connected to our partners not only by the feelings we had for them, but with the ideas about our relationships to them. When we disconnect, we have the dual task of unplugging our feelings as well as disconnecting from our ideas about our relationships and feelings about those ideas. Only then can we properly focus our concerns about being alone and learn to endure the accompanying feelings. Only then will we find the path for normal grief, thus avoiding the despair of melancholia.

This chapter teaches how to grieve normally for the departed others. We shall learn how to give the departed a proper burial. We shall learn how to cover the corpses of their broken promises by filling the shallow graves of their reassurances that "tomorrow will be different" with the earth of normal grief. We shall learn that mourning can end and need not become melancholia.

You can survive a broken relationship. That genius of the human predicament, Sigmund Freud, described the critical distinction between normal grieving and pathological melancholia or depression after loss in his 1917 paper, "Mourning and Melancholia."

"It's a matter of general observation," he noted, "that people never willingly abandon a libidinal position even when a substitute is beckoning to them." Put more simply, people never say goodbye easily, even when somebody else is there and waiting.

He went on to say, "Mourning is the normal reaction to the loss of a loved person, but in some people the same losses produce melancholia which is distinguished from normal grieving by a profoundly painful dejection, cessation of interest in the outside world, inhibition of activity, the lowering of self-esteem, self-accusation and the expectations of punishment."

He then made this critical crossover point from psychodynamic theory to that practical insight which provides the rationale for this closing chapter. He said, "If one listens patiently to a melancholic's many and various self-accusations, one cannot in the end avoid the impression that with insignificant modification they fit someone else. For we have also long known that no one harbors thoughts of suicide or self-destructiveness which he has not derived from murderous or other hostile impulses against others." That's the key! The loss or threat of loss of a loved object provides unparalleled opportunity for examining the ambivalence of that relationship, vis à vis its hostile elements!

Comprehending the meaning of this concept of ambivalence is one of the most difficult tasks for the psychiatry resident. The reason for this is that before it could be seen, denial and doubt of its presence had first to be overcome.

"You must be crazy yourself, doctor," mutters the bereaved widow, "to think that I am angry with my always devoted and now deceased husband who did everything for me; who wouldn't let me lift a finger; who wrote every check; who never burdened me with news of our finances and protected me from anything which would distress me!"

But we who stand one decibel or two removed from the manifest notes of her description of their relationship, hear her also say, "How could he do this to me? How dare he die and leave me? I hate my life without him and I hate him for making it so, not only now, but then too. I hated my inadequacy, and him for sponsoring it." His death let in the news of her diminished self-worth and she is angry with this discovery. But it was there all the time, just denied.

Another example may further clarify this point about repressed anger and denied hostility, during this widow's bereavement in particular and the role of ambivalence in human relationships in general.

Poor phobic Mary could never go on business trips with her husband, whose infidelity while on them she practically choreographed. Knowing this, she could maintain her sexual frigidity, which of course also protected her from expressing more directly her anger with her faithless husband. His anger, on the other hand, with her silly rationalization of needing to protect herself from germs on airplanes justified not only his affairs, but taking promotions in her father's company which others, by talent and longevity should have received long before him.

I wish this were just psychobabble and psychoanalytic mumbo jumbo. However, you only have to sit in divorce court for one afternoon to see what was once a caring commitment and agreement putrefy into hate and resentment. But that hate was not de novo created that day, but was a regression to the uncivilized child whose ambivalence untempered by the reality principle has erupted because someone didn't get what they wanted when they wanted it.

What most folks thought they saw in their early relationships is not what they got. What they too often saw was the veneer of bluff and denial. What so many couples soon inherited after their honeymoons were over was the legacy of the unresolved underlying interpersonal hostilities and inabilities in their partners to let reality prevail where childish wishes and entitlements once reigned.

What they have are neurotic relationships where ambivalence is rabid and sublimation has no footing.

Of the forces that underlie all human relationships, i.e., amity, caring and union, with reassurance and affirmation of the partner as its mode, the second destructive force of mastery and conquest with maneuver and control as its mode has prevailed. In the secure and well balanced relationship, those latter forces sublimate to overprotectiveness, honest worry, rational discipline and normal anger, with disappointment and displeasure as its downside emotions. In bitching unions, however, even the slightest negative stimulus can ignite repressed, denied, and foresworn hostile forces. Those immature partners cannot abide the simplest trespass of their perceived needs. The mechanism is simple. First they idealize their worth and then assert their narcissistic entitlement to the perfect devotion of their partners. They do not countenance such normal feelings as peeving and disappointment. For them, all disappointment and imminent threats of loss uncap their infantile helplessness. They are cradled in the prison of their primitive pasts. They want what they want when they want it, and damned be those who first cry "No!" Frustration of today's simple hunger or thirst for attention transforms almost chemically into a rediscovery of all dormant anger and all disappointment unresolved from the dawn of their history.

Those so insecure are intolerant of even the slightest violation of their presumed entitlements. They have no filter to contain yesterday's rage from today's disappointment. Our failures are unforgivable, not for the reality of our present limitations, but because they are reminders. We are only triggers of preloaded, pointed weapons.

Even more sadly, this wrath can be and often is turned against themselves by the mechanism of defense called introjection, first described in Chapter 6. Those "bad others" from both the past and present are introjected. Then, as Freud so precisely pointed out, "The complaints of the melancholic are really plaints in the old sense of the word. For everything derogatory that they say about themselves in their melancholia, they have said about those others before they were lost." By introjection, they now exist within. So, just as they could not forgive them in real life, they cannot now forgive them in death or loss.

At some critical point in the furthest interiors of the immature partner's central nervous system, rage at others or depression and self-depreciation are precariously juxtaposed. By this psychodynamic mechanism of introjection, one can become the other in an instant. For us their partners, however, it makes little practical difference which prevails. In either case, we are in the fallout of their neurotic travail.

If this chapter did no more than elucidate the juxtapositioning of rage against others, either overt or neurotically disguised as depression with self-depreciation of the self, it would have served a valuable purpose. However, we can proceed further with this knowledge and advance our discourse on what to do next. First these critical questions must be answered: Could it be that I am describing you and not them? Could it be that you are the partner I was just talking about? Could it be that you are the bitcher and they are hitched to your past?

One of my most admired teachers, Elvin Semrad, once said, "Most couples deserve each other." He was the same mentor whose "Folks will be folks" aphorism hangs on my waiting room wall, nicely framed and embroidered on white linen. I guess that observation heralded the great to-do which is being made these days about enablers. This phenomenon was first addressed as it related to spouses or adult children of alcoholics. Now, however, it has found its way even into so-called "pop" psychotherapy seminars where the lecturer admonishes the audience about our giving or not giving them the space in our lives to continue not to change. The real point, however, is that in the ambivalent relationships of immature people there occurs, after a while, a regressive balance. Whether it takes the form of the enabling of one partner to regress by participating passively in his aggressive behaviors against you or self-destructive behaviors against himself is almost moot. What is not moot is that there is no more reliable measure for having a satisfactory and mature adult relationship than to note the way our partners have dealt with the inevitable losses and disappointments inherent in all human development.

In my work at county jails and prisons, I learned a great deal about the criminal mind and the complexity of meting out a proper punishment, but no truth was more impressive than this one:

"Don't do the crime if you can't do the time." Its wisdom is pervasive, especially in this more universal application:

"Don't play the game if you can't lose."

"Don't connect if you can't separate."

These samples from the local newspaper demonstrate this point: a critique of the film *Dangerous Liaisons* and a front page story of a woman murdered by a felon recently released from our state correctional system who could not abide the news that time had cooled her ardor for his plans for "starting up again."

I see it all too often in my patients' divorces and custody fights. Next week I will testify in two custody cases, in which four preschoolers are caught in the crossfire of verbal child abuse as acrimonious parents shout invectives so loud that neither can hear the weeping of their children nor take measure of the dire consequences which their unrepressed ambivalence will visit upon them.

But how, you may ask, do we know if we are sore losers, if we have never lost anything? First, by correcting that fallacy. We all have lost something. We have lost our entitlements to infantile attention and care. We have lost our innocence. We have lost our entitlement to quids for which no quos are required. We have lost the reality of someone else being responsible for us. We have lost the right to receive without giving. We have lost the prerogative to not share in our relationships.

Yes, but have we lost the fantasy of it, and do we still behave as if it were so? The answer can be found in how we play the game of our adult relationships.

Let me give you an example of this from my personal past. No patient stories this time—one from the Doc himself!

Between my second and third years of medical school, I was very much in love with a coed whose summer plans took her to a job in a union camp in Pennsylvania, while mine took me to a waiter's job on the Massachusetts Northshore. We corresponded with zeal, if not poetry, for three quarters of the summer, and each of us presumably with the same anticipation for our rendezvous the week before classes were to resume. However, when she decided to take the train home, rather than have me pick her up, I knew something was amiss. Sure enough, there was, in the form of a basketball player from Scranton who apparently suffered more with the world's woes than I did and could sink jump shots with a better consistency.

As she hemmed and hawed about how best to let me know and let me go, she wept, "Well, you know, Alfred, I've never really seen you in stress." What she meant, I guess, was, "How can I actually say I know you or how can I really love you without knowing this."

Dammit, if she didn't hit the nail on the head, and to this day I am very grateful to dear J.B. Life has given both of us an opportunity to have plenty of losses, and a careful measure of how we fared after them would certainly be helpful in knowing, if we were to meet again, whether we would then be a better match.

The first of those future stresses was dealing quite well, I thought, with her rejection. I promptly began dating the twin of my roommate's girlfriend, almost flunked my first semester of pathology, and lost my bar mitzvah fountain pen.

The, point of these anecdotes is really quite simple and was nicely exposited by the Gestalt therapist Fritz Perls, whose aphorisms dominated the pop psychology charts of the 1960s, i.e.,

"I am not here to please you … and you are not here to please me …" he taught. *"… and if we touch, so be it … and if we don't so what …"*

No relationship agreement can or should have to bear the weight of a preamble which says, "Don't come if you can't stay." This is not, of course, condoning arbitrary or deceitful departures after partners have been exploited or duped. I am referring to the inevitable discoveries of limit which all partners must learn to accept if space and resources are to be shared. However, most importantly, I am referring to each partner's right to assert limits to no longer forbear a union which yields less than aloneness.

However far relationships may take us to new vistas of communion and joy, they must never burn the bridge for either partner's safe return to his home alone, nor should they ever be undertaken until such a home exists. Yet we see many who have dared such journeys with no provision for a safe return. Some have left the safety of oneness to chance the journey to be in love or loved with no compass for their return trip. What is even worse is that others have begun the journey with self-doubt and self-depreciation, preferring to play the lottery for a bad relationship to staying home alone.

It is this terrible specter of a return to a fragile aloneness that seals the bitching communion. I suppose if you're gathering material for the great American novel, you can accept yourself in such a tragic comic role, but for most of us, it surely isn't worth it.

What most folks haven't appreciated is that just being better with someone, but okay without them, is the true grail of interpersonal success. Whether we call it an I/thou relationship and subscribe to the teachings of Martin Buber or love according to Eric Fromm, makes little difference. What makes it work is mastery of solitude, being able to be okay alone first, then better with someone.

Let me elaborate on "being with" someone. It sounds so simple, doesn't it? But try it. Try to separate from your needs and wishes for a few moments as you provide quiet audience for another. Explore a devotion to their existence. Can you truly pay attention and listen for a while, unfettered by your own coincidental or future needs? Can you play give and no take? Not forever, of course, but at least long enough to take measure of your partner's full human presence. How can you really ever know another if your antennae for perceiving them are impeded by the urgency of your own needs and desires?

Could it be that this is the true Biblical meaning of "knowing," and not the physical definition more conventionally attributed to that Biblical verb?

There is only one arena for interpersonal joy, and that is where two wholes unencumbered by need or self-inadequacy touch; not where parts glom to one another for balance or oneness.

Just recently I had an unusual opportunity to reflect further upon this matter. An attractive, bright and sensitive 41-year-old legal secretary was referred by a patient of mine, ostensibly with his permission to allow me to help her understand him. She was recently relieved by divorce of a 21-year marriage to a man with whom she protested she never "in all those 21 years had a tenth of the pleasure, laughter, reassurance or wellness feelings" which she had come to enjoy with her new lover. But she protested she was not happy, and that was the issue that brought her to her first visit. Was it real, or was it an act? Was she a player in a macabre scheme of exploitation, was she a character in his play or was it really happening?

Her friendly philosopher friends would say, "If it feels good, do it," but somehow that advice paled in the bright sun of a Florida morning. She wanted more than feeling good, but couldn't find the words for a more specific question. "Was it real or was it Memorex?" seemed too trite a question at this time. But there was no doubt that the glass was broken. "Am I just the latest in his stable of serial affairs?" she asked. "What do I really mean to him?"

After a proper acknowledgment of his permission to me to tell her what I knew about him (as a former patient), I politely denied that route of solution for her problem. I replied, "Better than, 'what do I really mean to him?'" she needed to ask, "What does he really mean to me?" To discover the answer to this question, she needed to answer these other questions: "How little can I know, how much must I know before we go further?"

After a pensive silence, she asked her own question: "Would I be a fool to learn to play the game of our relationship better than he? Do I demean us by calling our relationship a game?" I loved her questions. While treating neurosis is my cash crop, existential inquiry is the dessert of my practice. I'm sure my colleagues could have a field day with the more classic psychiatric components of this couple's relationship and could easily fit their dilemma into several clinical metaphors.

But for me the problem is existential. Can they accept each other as they are?

In the *Accidental Tourist,* Macon captures this point beautifully when he says, "It's not a matter of 'do we love each other?' It's 'can we be ourselves with one another?'"

When my former patient appeared for a second look at his life with this new ladyfriend, he began by saying, "Look Doc, I ain't deep. I only hurt people who want more from me than I can give, and I do my best with people who are OK without me. But I don't insist they stay if that's not OK for them." Which would, of course, not be unhitching from bitching but unhitching before bitching.

Unfortunately, there are all too few couples who will tarry with such an inquiry before union. For those who will, this book's message is one of prevention. For those who haven't, this book is for goodbye and rebirth.

Because my practice has become skewed so to consider troubled relationships rather than individual traits of neurosis, I talk less about curing and more about growing and learning. I don't promise health and well-being. I promise awareness, insight and mastery of previously unrealized limits and inadequacies. I promise that individuals will learn something about themselves in particular and relationships in general. This knowledge, I assert, will not only help master the distressing symptoms which prompted the seeking of help, but will enable a more fruitful harvest from interpersonal relationships. However, this critical caveat applies, "Only those who have the courage to leave, can find the wisdom to stay." Therapy provides choice for the former and insight for the latter.

The message of this book is the same. I hope readers have learned something about themselves in particular and their relationships in general, for that will surely be helpful in unhitching from bitching.

• • •

Alfred Fireman, MD
September 15, 1930 – October 13, 1998

Resume / Curriculum Vitae

35 years of clinical psychiatric practice

Undergraduate and Professional Education
Brown University, A.B. Cum Laude, Phi Beta Kappa, 9/48–6/52
Tufts University Medical School, M.D. Pfizer Scholarship, 9/52–6/56

Post Doctoral Training and Experience
Rotating Internship, King's County Hospital, Brooklyn, NY, 7/56–6/57
Resident in Psychiatry, Boston V.A. Hospital, 7/57–6/58
Resident in Psychiatry, Boston University Hospital, 7/58–6/59 and 7/61–6/62
Fellowship, National Endowment for the Humanities, University of Texas,
    Medical Ethics, Summer, 1976
Brown University Summer College, International Relations, 1980
Fellow, Kennedy Institute for Ethics, Georgetown, DC, Summer, 1981
Annual certified continuing medical education credits for 34 years (primarily in forensic
    psychiatry)

Certifications and Licensure
Diplomate of the National Board of Medical Examiners, 7/57
Diplomate of the American Board of Psychiatry and Neurology, 10/63
Medical Licensure: MA #26523, 1/61, and RI #3561, 6/62, inactive; FL #17915, 8/71,
    active (with certified CME credits until recertification due in 2001 (primarily secured
    in forensic psychiatry)

Prior Practice, Consultantships, Community Service, and Hospital Staff Appointments
Rhode Island, 1962–1971:
Staff Psychiatrist, Butler Hospital; Clinical Director, East Bay Counseling Center;
    Chairman, Mayor's Committee for Community Mental Health Planning; Senior
    Board Member, Community Mental Health Clinic; Planned Parenthood; Division of
    Vocational Rehabilitation; Model Cities Juvenile Delinquency Project; Marathon Drug
    Rehabilitation House; Major Corporate Personnel Departments; Tunisia Peace Corps
    Project; U.S. Department of Defense (Industrial Security Clearance Office), U.S. Navy
    War College

Florida, 1972–1996:
Psychiatrist-in-chief, University of South Florida Student Health and Counseling Cen-
    ter; Director, Alcohol and Drug Rehab Unit, Bay Pines V.A. Hospital; Private Practice
    of General Psychiatry with consultantships to Alzheimer's Information and Family
    Resource Center; The Institute for Rational Living (and their several sales promotion
    seminars); Agenda Marketing (an international timeshare organization); U.S. Coast
    Guard Air Station Dispensary and Pinellas County Homeless Center

Hospital Staff Appointments:
Psychiatric (1972–1996): Medfield, Horizon, Fairwinds
General (1972–1996): Largo Medical Center, Morton Plant, St. Petersburg General,
    Palms of Pasadena

Forensic Sub Specialization
Research Assistant for mentally disordered sex offenders, Walpole and Bridgewater State
    Prisons, MA, 1958
Residency Rotation, Boston University Law Medicine Institute, 1959
Eastern Regional Consultant to APA Committee on Corrections, 1959–61
Lieutenant, U.S. Navy, Chief Psychiatrist, Maximum Security Prison, Portsmouth, NH,
    1959–61
Director, Parole Clinic, Massachusetts Department of Mental Health, 1962
Consultant, Rhode Island Public Defender's and District Attorney's Offices, 1963–71
Forensic expert witness in State and Federal Courts of RI, NH, MA, and FL, from 1963
    to present
Consultant psychiatrist, Pinellas County Jail, 1975–83
Consultant, Florida Department of Professional Regulation, 1987–90

Publications and Presentations – Forensic
"Pre-Acute Crime Milieu," *Archives of Criminal Psychodynamics*, Spring, 1961. Abstracted
    in *Digest of Neurology and Psychiatry*, Hartford Institute

"A Psychiatrist Takes the Stand," *American Journal of Corrections*, 3/62

Leader, Rhode Island Conference of Social Work Annual Institutes, "Problems of
    Responsibility in Criminal Behavior," 1963 and 1964

"A Study of the Interaction Between Prisoners and Guards," *American Journal of Correc-
    tions*, Jan./Feb., 1963

"Problems of Criminal Responsibility," *Rhode Island Medical Journal*, 1/63. Abstracted in
    Excepta Medica Psychiatra

Discussant, John McDonald's paper, "The Threat to Kill," APA Meeting, St. Louis, MO,
    5/63

Editorial Viewpoint in *Florida Bar Journal*, "Dangerousness is Not a Medical Issue," Vol.
    51, No. 3, 3/77

"Confessions of a Forensic Psychiatrist," read at the 9th Annual Meeting of the Amer-
    ican Academy of Psychiatry and the Law, Montreal, Canada, 10/78, and published in
    the *American Journal of Forensic Psychiatry*, Vol. 1, No. 2, 2/79

"On the Use of Psychotropics in a County Jail," Workshop at AMA, Meetings on Correction Medicine,Chicago, IL, 10/80

CLE Symposium: "Challenging Psychiatric and Psychological Testimony," Atlanta, GA, 2/81; New Orleans, LA, 2/81; Pensacola, FL, 3/81 (primary speaker)

Producer/Director of 90-minute video documentary on the interface between crime and mental illness as portrayed in 11 clinical interviews with selected inmates at the Pinellas County Jail, presented at the American Medical Association Fifth National Conference on Medical Care and Health Services in Correctional Institutions, Chicago, IL, 10/81; revised and presented to the Society of Health and Human Values Southern Regional Meeting, Charleston, SC, Medical School, Spring, 1982

"A Study of the Health Care Services at the Pinellas County Jail, Clearwater, Florida," presented on contract to Pinellas County Commissioners, 2/83

"Update Report on the Use of Psychotropics in a Jail and Prison Setting," Second World Congress of Prison Health Care, Ottawa, Canada, 8/83

"A Study of the Relationship Between Crime and Mental Illness," presented at the American College of Forensic Psychiatry Annual Meeting, Sanibel Island, FL, 4/86

"Using Medical Expert Witnesses," CLER Lecture Program, Tampa and Miami, FL, 11/92

Publications and Presentations – Other
"An Experiment in Community Education," *Rhode Island Medical Journal*, 1/65. Read at APA Divisional Meeting, Philadelphia, PA, 11/65

"Socrates and Psychotherapy," read at APA Meeting, Atlantic City, NY, 5/66. Published in *Journal of Existential Psychiatry*, 1966. Abstracted in *Psychiatric Spectator*, Sandoz, 1966

"Industrial Psychiatry," Eleventh Annual University of Rhode Island Safety Institute, 1968 Panel Moderator, American Ontoanalytic Meeting, Boston, MA, 5/68; topic: "Existential Psychiatry." Discussants: A. Maslow, William Barrett, Stanley Diamond

"Toward a Unitary Principle of Self," read at American Ontoanalytic Association Meeting, 5/71

"Recreation Phobia," *Recreation Management*, Volume 16, No. 3, 4/73

"The Role of a Psychiatrist in a University Health and Counseling Center," *Journal of the Florida Medical Association*, 10/73. Read at SE Conference on Counseling Personnel, St. Petersburg, FL, 10/73

Congress of Recreation and Parks (NPRA). Panel and workshop speaker with Jonathan Kozol and Margaret Mead. Topic: "Redefining Leisure," 10/73

"What is Existential Psychiatry?" Florida Psychiatric Society, Fall Meeting, 1975

"Sex and Love" [essay], presented to the Florida Psychiatric Association Annual Meeting, Tampa, FL, 11/82

"Mental and Emotional Illnesses Induced by Physical Trauma," Annual Meeting of the Clearwater Bar Association, Clearwater, FL, 4/85

Research and Survey Report for Health and Retirement Corporation of America on the need for a new Alzheimer's nursing home in Pinellas and Pasco Counties, FL, 3/87

"Bodyowners' Insurance: A Better Answer to the [Medical] Mispractice Crisis," *Florida Underwriter Magazine*, Vol. 7, #6, 6/90

"A Psychiatrist Talks About Love," *Psychiatric Times*, Summer, 1992

"Against Ambiguity: An Homage to Knowledgeable Love," *The Progressive Women's Quarterly*, Spring, 1993

"Obesity is Not a Psychiatric Illness," 45th Annual Symposium of the American Society of Bariatric Physicians, San Diego, CA, 11/16/95; and excerpted in PICOMESO (Pinellas County Medical Society) *Mailbag*, 2/96

Legislature Assignments
Rhode Island: Topic: Revision of the Rhode Island NGRI Statute
Florida: Topic: Revision of the Mentally Disordered Sex Offender Statute

Teaching
"Medical Psychology," Brown University Extension School, 1965
"The Psychology of Marriage," University of Rhode Island, 1970
"Group Psychodynamics," Brown University, 1971
"Psychodynamic Medicine" seminars with residents of Mariam and Rhode Island Hospitals, 1968–70
Psychiatric Supervisor of Psychology Ph.D. candidates, University of Rhode Island, 1968–70
Lecturer in "Abnormal Psychology" and "Leisure Studies," University of South Florida, Tampa, FL, 1972
Visiting faculty, St. Leo College, Brooksville, FL, "Personality Theory and the Criminal Mind," 1975–76
Lecturer in Neurophysiology, Argenbright International Institute of Polygraphy, St. Petersburg, FL, 5–7/85

Present Agenda of Expert Testimony
Physician Assisted Suicide, Florida Hemlock Society
Death Sentence Review, Office of the Capital Collateral Representative, Tampa, FL
Munchausen Syndrome by Proxy, Florida, New York, South Dakota and Iowa
NGRI and Aid in Sentencing [including several capital cases], Florida's Sixth Judicial
    Circuit, Pinellas County

Mental Competency Evaluator, Florida Sixth Judicial Circuit

Media Experience
Frequent television and radio talk show appearances in Rhode Island and Florida
Featured contributor for articles on psychiatric issues in *Providence Journal* and *St.
    Petersburg Times*
20/20 Show, consultant to producers, 1993
Guest, discussing Munchausen Syndrome (Disease) by Proxy and the cases he has
    defended on the *Phil Donahue Show*, 5/14/92, https://www.youtube.com
    /watch?v=rqLVA4FsBKs
Guest, discussing Munchausen Syndrome (Disease) by Proxy and the cases he has
    defended, *Geraldo Rivera Show*, 5/25/93, https://www.youtube.com/watch?v
    =HsVdSCnhUkM
Alfred E. Fireman MD, discusses Women's Rights and Delinquency on Ring Around
    Rhode Island, in the mid 1960s, https://www.youtube.com/watch?v=w1imAHBe-VI

• • •

A Word from Payton Fireman, Dr. Fireman's Son

The resume/curriculum vitae above gives a structured sense of Alfred's accomplishments but comes nowhere close to describing the passion and compassion which he brought to his practice and his patients.

I remember Alfred rising early and leaving the house before dawn, to go to the county jail. He went to evaluate prisoners showing signs of mental illness and to bring his skills to the most unfortunate and least regarded. He used the first and best energies of his day to treat the sick and the disordered in the dungeons of our society. By his presence as witness, and with his authority as a physician, he helped ensure that the mentally ill would not suffer more in jail because of their infirmity. He stood guard in those places of misery to ameliorate the suffering and reduce the trauma of jail time. Before he saw the people who could pay him, he brought his skills to those who could not.

Alfred also had a great sense of humor as the accompanying picture clearly shows.

www.ingramcontent.com/pod-product-compliance
Lightning Source LLC
Chambersburg PA
CBHW032115280326
41933CB00009B/854